AF450286

FLUSHED WITH KNOWLEDGE

100 TRIVIA FACTS FOR YOUR TIME ON THE THRONE

Compiled and published by Christos Poulakis

FLUSHED WITH KNOWLEDGE
100 TRIVIA FACTS FOR YOUR TIME ON THE THRONE

First edition: July 2023

Compiled and published by **Christos Poulakis**
Cover designed by **Burcu Taşkin**

© 2023, Christos Poulakis

ISBN: 978-618-86745-0-9

CONTENTS

To Phoebus

INTRODUCTION

Toilets are a ubiquitous part of modern life, yet we often take them for granted. They provide us with a private moment of peace and reflection, and in this moment, our minds wander to unexpected places. Imagine if you could use this time to learn something maybe new and fascinating, something that will enrich your understanding of the world and impress your friends with your newfound knowledge.

That is the aim of this book, *FLUSHED WITH KNOWLEDGE: 100 TRIVIA FACTS FOR YOUR TIME ON THE THRONE;* in these pages, you will find a curated collection of the most interesting, surprising, and often bizarre facts from a wide range of topics. From science and history to fashion and art, these facts are sure to captivate your attention and leave you wanting to know more.

In addition to providing 100 interesting and often little-known trivia facts from 20 categories, *FLUSHED WITH KNOWLEDGE* goes one step further by including a QR code for each fact that takes you directly to its corresponding Wikipedia page, allowing you to delve even deeper into the topic.

So, whether you're looking to impress your friends with your vast array of knowledge, entertain yourself during a bathroom break, or simply expand your horizons, *FLUSHED WITH KNOWLEDGE* is the perfect companion. Just sit back, relax, and prepare to be amazed by the incredible world around us!

1. HISTORY

1. The first recorded instance of toilet paper use was in China in the 6th century CE.

The first recorded use of toilet paper in China in the 6th century CE was actually quite different from the toilet paper we know today. Instead of the soft, fluffy rolls we use now, it was more like a rough, flat sheet made of materials such as hemp and mulberry bark. At the time, the use of toilet paper was primarily limited to the wealthy and elite members of Chinese society, with many people still relying on other methods such as water or leaves. It wasn't until the 14th century that toilet paper began to be produced on a larger scale and become more widely used throughout China. Interestingly, it wasn't until the late 19th century that toilet paper use became more common in Western countries, with many people still relying on alternatives such as newspapers and catalogs well into the early 20th century. Today, toilet paper is considered a necessity for most people around the world and is produced and consumed on a massive scale. And just like that, what was once a luxury item for the wealthy has become a household staple that we just can't live without - talk about a bum deal!

2. The youngest person to ever become a monarch was King Oyo of Toro, who ascended to the throne of the Kingdom of Toro in Uganda at the age of just 3 years old.

King Oyo of Toro, whose full name is Rukidi IV Oyo Nyimba Kabamba Iguru Rukidi IV, was born on April 16, 1992, in Fort Portal, Uganda. He became king in 1995 after the death of his father, King Patrick David Matthew Kaboyo Olimi III. His coronation was held in 1996 when he was just 3 years old, making him the youngest monarch in the world at that time. The Kingdom of Toro is a traditional kingdom in Uganda that has a cultural and ceremonial role, and is not involved in the country's political system. Despite his young age, King Oyo had a team of advisors who helped him with his duties as a monarch. He was also educated at a boarding school in the United Kingdom and later went on to study at the University of Winchester in England. In 2009, he received a degree in Social and Economic Studies. As king, King Oyo has been a strong advocate for education and has launched initiatives to improve the quality of education in his kingdom. He has also been involved in efforts to promote tourism in the region and has worked to preserve the cultural heritage of the Toro people. In 2010, he founded the Tooro Kingdom Education Fund, which provides scholarships to underprivileged children in his kingdom. Despite being one of the youngest monarchs in history, King Oyo's reign has been far from child's play!

3.   The shortest war in history lasted only 38 minutes between the countries of Zanzibar and the United Kingdom in 1896.

The Anglo-Zanzibar War of 1896 was a brief military conflict that took place between the United Kingdom and the Sultanate of Zanzibar on August 27, 1896. It is considered the shortest war in history as it lasted only 38 minutes. The conflict started when the British consul demanded that the new Sultan, Khalid bin Barghash, should step down and allow the British preferred candidate to take over. However, Khalid refused to abdicate and instead took refuge in the palace. The British responded by sending warships to the harbor and bombarding the palace, while Zanzibar's defense forces responded with their own artillery. However, the Sultan's forces were vastly outnumbered and outgunned. After just 38 minutes of fighting, the Sultan's forces suffered heavy casualties, with around 500 soldiers and civilians killed or injured. The palace was also heavily damaged by the British bombardment. The war ended when the Sultan's forces surrendered, and he was forced to flee into exile. The British quickly installed their preferred candidate, Hamoud bin Mohammed, as the new Sultan. The conflict had little impact beyond Zanzibar itself, but it remains a fascinating historical footnote due to its brief duration. It probably took longer to declare war than it did to actually fight it!

4.   The Black Death, which killed an estimated 75-200 million people in Eurasia during the 14th century, was caused by the Yersinia pestis bacterium, which is still present in some parts of the world today.

The Black Death, also known as the bubonic plague, was one of the deadliest pandemics in human history. It originated in China and spread across Asia, the Middle East, and Europe, carried by fleas that infested rats. The Yersinia pestis bacterium, which caused the disease, could be transmitted from person to person through respiratory droplets or through bites from infected fleas. The symptoms of the disease included fever, chills, body aches, and the appearance of painful, swollen lymph nodes called buboes. In some cases, the disease progressed to septicemia, which could cause the skin to turn black and lead to death within days. The outbreak of the Black Death in Europe in the mid-14th century had a profound impact on European society. The mortality rate was so high that it disrupted the social order, with entire villages and towns being depopulated. The labor shortage that resulted from the pandemic led to higher wages for workers, while the loss of population reduced the demand for food and other goods, causing prices to fall. Although the Black Death is often associated with the 14th century, the Yersinia pestis bacterium still exists today and can cause outbreaks of the disease in some parts of the world. The continued presence of the bacterium serves as a reminder of the devastating impact that pandemics can have on human populations. And that's why it's always a good idea to keep your distance from rats and fleas, folks!

5.   The first telephone book was only one page long and contained only 50 names.

The first telephone book was published in 1878 in New Haven, Connecticut, by the New Haven District Telephone Company. This telephone book was only one page long and contained a total of 50 names. The purpose of the telephone book was to help people find other individuals or businesses that had telephones. The first telephone book was very different from the phone books we have today. It was printed on a single sheet of paper, and the names were listed in alphabetical order with no phone numbers included. Instead, people were expected to know the phone number of the person they wanted to call or to ask the operator for assistance. As telephones became more popular, telephone books began to expand. By the early 1900s, telephone books were typically several pages long and contained hundreds of names. In 1928, the first Yellow Pages directory was created, which listed businesses by category and helped people find local businesses more easily. Today, telephone books have largely been replaced by online directories and search engines, such as Google and Bing. While some telephone companies still print paper directories, they are often smaller in size and distributed only to customers who request them. And just like that, the phone book went from being a household staple to a doorstop!

2. SCIENCE

6.   The smallest known particle is the quark, which is a fundamental component of protons and neutrons.

The concept of the quark was first proposed in 1964 by physicists Murray Gell-Mann and George Zweig. They suggested that the protons and neutrons that make up the nucleus of an atom were themselves composed of smaller particles they called quarks. At first, the idea was not taken seriously by the scientific community, but over time, experimental evidence began to accumulate in support of the theory. Quarks are now widely accepted as one of the building blocks of matter, along with leptons and bosons. They come in six "flavors": up, down, charm, strange, top, and bottom. Protons and neutrons are made up of combinations of quarks, with each proton containing two "up" quarks and one "down" quark, and each neutron containing two "down" quarks and one "up" quark. Quarks are not found in isolation in nature, due to a phenomenon known as confinement. Because of their strong interaction with the strong nuclear force, quarks cannot be separated from each other, and instead exist only in combinations within larger particles. This is why they are called "fundamental particles" - they are not actually observable in isolation, but rather are inferred from their effects on other particles. Despite their small size and elusiveness, quarks have revolutionized our understanding of the structure of matter and the workings of the universe at the most fundamental level. So, remember, never judge someone by their size!

7. The human body contains approximately 30 000 trillion cells, each with a specific function, and the DNA in those cells can stretch around 2 meters (6 feet) if unraveled.

The human body is a marvel of biological engineering, and the sheer number of cells it contains is mind-boggling. Each cell in the body is a tiny, self-contained unit that performs a specific function necessary for the proper functioning of the body as a whole. There are many different types of cells, ranging from blood cells to nerve cells to muscle cells, each with a specific shape and function. In addition to their function, cells also contain genetic material in the form of DNA, which is responsible for determining an individual's physical characteristics and traits. DNA is organized into structures called chromosomes, which are located in the nucleus of the cell. Humans have 23 pairs of chromosomes, for a total of 46. The DNA in each cell is tightly packed into a structure called chromatin, which helps to protect and organize the genetic material. If the DNA in a single human cell were unraveled and stretched out in a straight line, it would measure around 2 meters (6 feet) long. However, since the DNA is tightly packed, it fits into the small space of the cell nucleus. It's interesting to note that while each cell in the human body contains the same genetic material, different cells use different portions of that DNA to perform their specific functions. For example, muscle cells use different parts of the DNA than skin cells or nerve cells. This specialization is what allows the body to function as a whole, with each cell playing its unique role in maintaining health and vitality. But don't worry, your DNA won't leave you hanging six feet apart!

8. The world's oldest known living organism is a 5,500-year-old tree named Methuselah, located in California's White Mountains. It was named after the biblical figure Methuselah, who was said to have lived for 969 years.

The Methuselah tree, a Great Basin bristlecone pine, was discovered in 1957 by Edmund Schulman, a renowned dendrochronologist who was studying the age of trees in the area. After analyzing Methuselah's growth rings, Schulman determined that the tree was over 4,800 years old at the time of its discovery, making it the oldest living organism known at the time. Since then, more accurate dating methods have been developed, and it has been determined that the tree is actually over 5,000 years old, with an estimated birthdate around 2832 BCE. Despite being thousands of years old, Methuselah is still growing, albeit very slowly. The harsh growing conditions at its high-altitude location have caused it to grow at a rate of only one inch in diameter every 100 years, resulting in a gnarled and twisted appearance. In order to protect Methuselah from damage, its exact location has been kept secret by the United States Forest Service. However, a nearby grove of similarly aged bristlecone pines known as the Patriarch Grove is open to the public and offers visitors a glimpse into the incredible world of these ancient trees. By analyzing the tree's growth rings, researchers have been able to reconstruct past weather patterns and gain a better understanding of how ecosystems have evolved over the centuries. So if you're ever looking for a good example of someone who's old and still growing, look no further than Methuselah the tree!

9. When a person blushes, not only their face but their entire body turns red. This is because the blood vessels all over the body dilate, causing an increase in blood flow.

Blushing is a physiological response that occurs when a person is embarrassed, anxious, or emotionally aroused. It is a form of nonverbal communication and can be an involuntary response to a perceived threat or social situation. When a person blushes, their body releases adrenaline, which causes the blood vessels in their face and other parts of their body to widen or dilate. This dilation allows more blood to flow through the vessels, causing the skin to turn red. Blushing is controlled by the sympathetic nervous system, which is responsible for the body's fight or flight response. The sympathetic nervous system reacts to emotional stimuli by causing the release of adrenaline, which increases heart rate and blood pressure. This, in turn, causes the blood vessels to dilate, leading to increased blood flow and a reddening of the skin. Interestingly, blushing can also be caused by other factors, such as heat, exercise, or alcohol consumption. In these cases, the blushing occurs due to an increase in body temperature or dilation of the blood vessels caused by alcohol. However, these types of blushing do not have the same emotional component as blushing due to embarrassment or anxiety. While blushing can be an uncomfortable experience for some people, it is a normal physiological response and usually harmless. So, the next time you feel yourself blushing, know that it's just your body's way of reacting to a social or emotional situation, and that it's perfectly normal!

**10.   The speed of light in a vacuum is approximately
300,000 kilometers per second (186,000 miles per second),
which is a fundamental constant of nature.**

The speed of light in a vacuum is one of the most important constants of nature and plays a crucial role in many scientific fields, including physics, astronomy, and engineering. It is also a fundamental part of Einstein's theory of relativity, which revolutionized our understanding of space and time. The speed of light is approximately 300,000 kilometers per second (186,000 miles per second), which is an astonishingly high speed. To put this in perspective, light can travel around the Earth's equator in just 1/7th of a second, or from the Earth to the moon in just 1.28 seconds. It is also the universal speed limit, meaning that nothing in the universe can travel faster than the speed of light. The speed of light is also a critical factor in the study of cosmology, the study of the origin and evolution of the universe. Astronomers use the speed of light to measure the distance of objects in space, such as galaxies and stars. They also use it to study the early universe, as light from the early universe can provide clues about the universe's formation and evolution. In addition to its importance in astronomy and physics, the speed of light has practical applications in everyday life. It is used in telecommunications, as light travels through fiber optic cables to transmit information quickly and efficiently. It is also used in medical imaging technologies such as X-rays and MRI machines, which use light waves to create detailed images of the body. And yet, despite its incredible importance, the speed of light still struggles to outrun the snail's pace of bureaucracy!

3. BUSINESS & ECONOMICS

11. The world's largest employer in the world is the American company Walmart, Inc., which employs over 2 million people.

Walmart, Inc. is a multinational retail corporation that operates a chain of hypermarkets, discount department stores, and grocery stores across the world. Founded in 1962 by Sam Walton, Walmart is headquartered in Bentonville, Arkansas, and has grown to become the largest company by revenue in the world. As of 2021, Walmart operates over 11,000 stores in 27 countries and employs more than 2.3 million associates worldwide. Walmart's workforce includes a diverse range of employees, including part-time workers, full-time workers, hourly employees, and salaried employees. In addition to its vast workforce, Walmart is also one of the world's largest companies by revenue, with annual revenue of over $500 billion. The company's success can be attributed to its low prices, wide selection of products, and efficient supply chain management. However, Walmart has also faced criticism over the years, particularly regarding its labor practices and treatment of workers. The company has been accused of paying low wages, offering limited benefits, and engaging in anti-union activities. Despite that, with over 2.3 million employees Walmart could practically form its own country, and with annual revenue of over $500 billion, it would probably be a wealthy one at that!

12. The world's first vending machine was invented in first-century Roman Egypt. It was a simple device that dispensed holy water in exchange for a coin.

The earliest known example of a vending machine dates back to the first century AD in Alexandria, Egypt. This machine, invented by a mathematician and engineer named Hero of Alexandria, was known as a "coin-operated holy water dispenser" and worked by using a lever to dispense holy water after a coin was inserted into the machine. The machine's design was based on a simple set of mechanics that allowed it to operate without any external source of power. The use of vending machines soon spread throughout the Roman Empire, where they were used to dispense a variety of products, including wine, olive oil, and spices. Today, vending machines have become ubiquitous, and can be found in almost every corner of the world, dispensing everything from snacks and beverages to electronics and even cars. They also incorporate advanced technologies such as touchscreens, credit card readers, and mobile payment systems, making them more user-friendly and accessible to a wider audience. Vending machines are used in a variety of settings, including schools, hospitals, airports, and train stations, and are an essential part of the retail industry. But be careful, don't get too excited when buying a car from a vending machine, or you might accidentally select the snack size option!

13. The world's oldest surviving bank is Monte dei Paschi di Siena, which was founded in Italy in 1472.

Monte dei Paschi di Siena (MPS) is not only the oldest surviving bank in the world, but it is also one of the most important banks in Italy. The bank was founded in Siena, Italy in 1472, during the Renaissance period. At that time, it was called Monte di Pietà, which was a non-profit organization that provided loans to those in need. The bank's original mission was to help people in financial difficulty, especially those who could not afford to borrow from private lenders, and to combat the practice of usury, which was widespread at the time. Over the centuries, the bank's mission evolved, and it eventually became a commercial bank. Today, MPS is a large Italian banking group, and it is still headquartered in Siena. The bank has branches throughout Italy and has expanded into other countries, including the United States, the United Kingdom, and China. MPS has had a tumultuous history, especially in recent years. In 2013, the bank was at the center of a financial scandal involving the sale of complex financial instruments to small Italian towns. The scandal led to the resignation of several top executives and a government bailout. In 2020, the bank was acquired by Italy's second-largest bank, UniCredit, after it struggled with mounting losses and bad loans. Despite its turbulent history, the fact that Monte dei Paschi di Siena has survived for more than five centuries is a testament to its resilience and enduring importance in the history of banking. And to think, all this time we've been worrying about the stability of our banks, when the real secret to success was just to start in the 15th century!

14.   The first credit card was introduced in 1950 by the Diners Club, a company founded by businessman Frank McNamara. The card was initially only accepted at 27 restaurants in New York City.

The introduction of the first credit card by Diners Club in 1950 revolutionized the way consumers paid for goods and services. Before the advent of credit cards, consumers had to carry cash or checks, which could be inconvenient and risky. Diners Club's credit card, initially designed as a way for businessmen to entertain clients at restaurants, allowed cardholders to charge their meals and pay for them later. The concept quickly caught on, and by the end of 1950, Diners Club had issued 10,000 cards and expanded its acceptance to more than 200 restaurants across the United States. Other credit card companies soon followed suit, including American Express, which introduced its own credit card in 1958. The credit card industry continued to grow throughout the 1960s and 1970s, with the advent of magnetic strip technology and the creation of the first national credit card network, MasterCharge (now known as Mastercard). Today, credit cards are ubiquitous, with millions of people around the world using them to make purchases both in person and online. Credit cards offer consumers convenience and flexibility, allowing them to make purchases and pay for them over time. However, credit cards can also come with high interest rates and fees, and carrying too much credit card debt can be detrimental to one's financial health. Just remember to always read the fine print before signing up for a credit card - or you might end up charging yourself into bankruptcy!

15. The world's oldest continuously operating family business is a Japanese construction company called Kongo Gumi, which was founded in 578 AD and has been run by the same family for over 1,400 years.

Kongo Gumi is a Japanese construction company that specializes in building Buddhist temples. The company was founded in 578 AD by a Korean immigrant named Shigemitsu Kongo, who was invited to Japan by Prince Shotoku to build the country's first Buddhist temple. Kongo Gumi has been passed down through the Kongo family for over 1,400 years, and has survived numerous wars, economic crises, and natural disasters, including earthquakes, typhoons, and fires. Throughout its long history, Kongo Gumi has built many of Japan's most famous temples, including the original construction of the Shitennoji Temple in Osaka. In addition to building temples, the company has also expanded into other areas of construction, such as commercial buildings and public works projects. Despite its long and storied history, Kongo Gumi faced financial difficulties in the early 2000s due to Japan's economic downturn and increasing competition in the construction industry. In 2006, the company was acquired by the Takamatsu Construction Group, ending its status as a family-owned business. However, the Kongo family continues to play an active role in the company's operations, and the Kongo Gumi name and legacy live on. It seems like Kongo Gumi really built their business to last, even surviving earthquakes and fires that could have put a serious dent in their construction plans - I guess you could say they're the original "masters of disaster"!

4. ARCHITECTURE & DESIGN

16. The world's tallest building is the Burj Khalifa in Dubai, standing at a height of 829.8 m (2,722 ft).

The Burj Khalifa, located in Dubai, United Arab Emirates, is an iconic skyscraper that opened in 2010 and stands as the tallest building in the world. It was designed by the Chicago-based architectural firm Skidmore, Owings & Merrill (SOM) and cost an estimated $1.5 billion to construct. The building's height of 829.8 meters (2,722 feet) is more than twice the height of the Empire State Building in New York City and approximately one and a half times the height of the World Trade Center buildings destroyed in the 9/11 terrorist attacks. The Burj Khalifa is a mixed-use development, meaning it contains a combination of uses such as residential, commercial, and hospitality. The building has 163 floors, which include luxury apartments, corporate offices, hotels, and restaurants. The top floor of the building houses the observation deck, which offers breathtaking views of Dubai and the surrounding desert. The building's exterior features a unique Y-shaped design, which maximizes the amount of natural light entering each unit. The Burj Khalifa has won numerous awards for its innovative design and engineering and has also become a symbol of modern Dubai and a major tourist attraction, drawing millions of visitors each year. Despite its impressive height, the Burj Khalifa still cannot escape one of life's most annoying problems: the wait for the elevator!

17. The famous Taj Mahal in Agra, India was built by Mughal Emperor Shah Jahan in memory of his beloved wife Mumtaz Mahal, who died in 1631.

The Taj Mahal is widely regarded as one of the greatest examples of Mughal architecture, a style that combines elements from Persian, Indian, and Islamic design. The monument was commissioned by Shah Jahan in 1632 and was completed in 1653, although some parts of the complex were not finished until several years later. The building's design is said to have been inspired by various architectural styles, including Persian, Indian, and Islamic motifs, and it features intricate carvings and inlays made of precious stones and materials such as marble and jade. The Taj Mahal is renowned for its impressive size and intricate details, as well as its stunning symmetry, which is particularly evident when viewed from certain angles. The construction of the Taj Mahal required a significant amount of resources, including a large workforce of skilled artisans, architects, and laborers. Estimates suggest that up to 20,000 workers were involved in the project at its peak, with many of them being recruited from nearby villages and towns. The construction also required the use of a wide range of materials, including marble, sandstone, and various precious stones, which were sourced from different parts of India and abroad. The entire complex, including the main mausoleum, surrounding gardens, and various support buildings, covers an area of around 42 acres. It's no wonder the Taj Mahal is considered one of the seven wonders of the world. With all those precious stones and intricate carvings, it's basically the world's largest and most expensive wedding gift!

18.   The Eiffel Tower, located in Paris, France, was originally built as a temporary structure for the 1889 World's Fair. It was almost dismantled after the fair, but was saved because it proved useful as a radio communications tower.

The Eiffel Tower was designed and built by Gustave Eiffel, a French engineer and entrepreneur, and his team of engineers and architects. Construction of the tower began in 1887 and was completed in just over two years. The tower was intended to showcase France's engineering prowess and was the center-piece of the 1889 World's Fair, which celebrated the 100th anniversary of the French Revolution. At the time, the tower was the tallest structure in the world, standing at a height of 324 meters (1,063 feet). After the World's Fair ended, the Eiffel Tower was almost dismantled due to its temporary nature. However, it was saved from destruction when it was discovered that the tower was well-suited for use as a radio communications tower. In 1900, a radio antenna was installed on the tower, which allowed it to transmit radio signals across the city and beyond. During World War I, the tower was also used for intercepting enemy radio communications. Today, the Eiffel Tower remains one of the most recognizable landmarks in the world and attracts millions of visitors each year. The tower has been the subject of numerous artistic works, including paintings, photographs, and films. But did you know that the Eiffel Tower was actually supposed to be a bit taller? Maybe it's a good thing they didn't go any higher, or else the Eiffel Tower might have been leaning like the Tower of Pisa!

19. The Great Wall of China, built over 2,000 years ago, is considered to be one of the greatest architectural achievements in history. However, despite popular belief, it cannot be seen from space with the naked eye.

The Great Wall of China is a series of fortifications built along the northern borders of China to protect against invasions and raids from various nomadic groups. Construction of the wall began in the 7th century BC and continued for many centuries, with each dynasty adding their own sections. The wall was built with a variety of materials, including brick, tamped earth, stone, and wood. It stretches over 21,000 kilometers (13,000 miles) and is the longest wall in the world. While the Great Wall of China is undoubtedly an impressive feat of engineering and architecture, the popular belief that it can be seen from space with the naked eye is not true. In fact, NASA astronauts have reported that it is nearly impossible to see the wall from space without aid, and even then, it is very difficult. This is because the wall is not wide enough to be visible from space and is not a single, continuous structure but rather a series of walls and fortifications that are broken up by mountains, hills, and other natural features. Despite this, the Great Wall of China remains one of the most popular tourist destinations in China and a symbol of the country's rich history and culture. Don't let the fact that you can't see it from space stop you from trying to spot it on your next flight though!

20. **The Parthenon temple in Athens, Greece was built without using any mortar. Instead, the builders used a technique called "dry stacking" in which the stones were cut and shaped so precisely that they fit together without the need for any adhesive material.**

The Parthenon temple in Athens, Greece is a Doric order temple dedicated to the goddess Athena. The construction of the temple began in 447 BC and took approximately 9 years to complete. The architects of the temple were Iktinos and Kallikrates, and the sculpture work was led by Phidias. The building materials for the Parthenon were marble from Mount Pentelicus, and the marble blocks were quarried and transported to the site using a network of ramps and pulleys. The technique of "dry stacking" was used by the builders to fit the marble blocks together without the use of mortar. The technique involved carving the blocks so precisely that they fit together tightly, creating a strong and stable structure. The precise fitting of the marble blocks was achieved through the use of measuring instruments such as the plumb line and level. Despite the impressive technique of "dry stacking," the Parthenon has been altered many times over the centuries through various modifications and restoration efforts, during which several original marble blocks were replaced. As a result, its present appearance differs significantly from the temple's initial form. The precise fitting of the marble blocks in the Parthenon was so perfect that not even a single drop of mortar was used, making it the original LEGO before the popular toy was even invented!

5. EDUCATION & ACADEMIA

21. The concept of letter grades (A, B, C, etc.) was first introduced in the United States in the late 19th century at Mount Holyoke College.

In the early years of formal education in the United States, there was no standardized system of grading students. Professors and teachers would simply provide comments or give students a pass or fail. However, this began to change in the late 19th century when Mount Holyoke College, a women's college in Massachusetts, introduced the concept of letter grades. This grading system was based on a 100-point scale and assigned letter grades ranging from A to F to indicate a student's performance. The system was quickly adopted by other colleges and universities across the United States. The letter grading system was seen as a more objective way to evaluate students and provide feedback on their academic performance. It also allowed for easier comparison of student performance across different courses and institutions. However, the system was not without its criticisms. Some argued that the letter grading system was too simplistic and did not provide enough detail on a student's strengths and weaknesses. Others criticized the system for placing too much emphasis on grades and not enough on the learning process itself. Despite these criticisms, the letter grading system remains the most widely used system of grading in the United States and many other countries. But don't worry, even if you got an F in a class, there's still hope for you to become an A-lister!

22. The first computer-based distance learning program was established in 1960 at the University of Illinois, using a system called PLATO (Programmed Logic for Automatic Teaching Operations).

The PLATO system was developed by a team of researchers led by Donald Bitzer, a computer scientist at the University of Illinois. It was initially created to provide computer-based instruction to students on campus, but its potential for distance learning quickly became apparent. The system allowed students to access course materials and interact with instructors and fellow students from remote locations, using a computer terminal connected to a mainframe computer. One of the key features of the PLATO system was its ability to provide interactive and engaging educational content, such as games and simulations, that went beyond traditional textbook-based learning. This approach to learning became known as computer-based instruction (CBI), which aimed to use technology to enhance and improve the learning process. Over the years, the PLATO system continued to evolve and expand, with new features and capabilities being added to enhance its functionality. By the late 1970s, it was being used by hundreds of educational institutions around the world, making it one of the most widely used distance learning systems of its time. The legacy of the PLATO system lives on, as it paved the way for the development of new technologies and approaches to learning that continue to shape the field of education and academia. Despite its success, there was one major flaw in the PLATO system - it didn't have a "mute" button, so students couldn't avoid the annoying kid in the virtual classroom!

23. In Finland, there are no mandated standardized tests for students until the age of 16, yet Finland's education system consistently ranks as one of the highest in the world.

Finland's education system is often cited as a model of success, and the lack of standardized testing is just one of its unique features. Instead of relying on standardized tests to measure student achievement and teacher effectiveness, Finland's education system places a strong emphasis on equity, equality, and individualized instruction. Teachers are highly trained and trusted to design their own curricula and assessments, based on the needs and interests of their students. The focus is on learning for its own sake, rather than on achieving high test scores or meeting prescribed standards. Another key element of Finland's education system is the strong social support provided to students and families. Students receive free meals, health care, and transportation to school, and there is a wide range of social services available to families, including child care and parental leave. This helps to level the playing field and ensure that all students have access to the resources and support they need to succeed. Additionally, Finland places a strong emphasis on early childhood education, recognizing that the foundation for lifelong learning is laid in the early years. Children are entitled to a free, high-quality preschool education, which focuses on play-based learning and social-emotional development. Despite the lack of standardized testing, Finland's education system consistently ranks among the highest in the world in terms of student achievement and equity. It just goes to show, sometimes less testing can lead to more success!

24. The idea of summer vacation for students in the United States originated from the agricultural calendar. Students were given a break during the summer months to help with farm work and harvest.

The practice of having a summer vacation for students in the United States has roots that can be traced back to the nation's agricultural history. In the 19th century, the vast majority of Americans lived in rural areas and worked in agriculture. During the summer months, children were needed to help with planting, tending to crops, and harvesting. Schools in rural areas often closed during this time, so that students could assist with the necessary agricultural work. This practice continued into the 20th century, even as more people began to move to urban areas and work in industries other than agriculture. The idea of summer vacation as a way to support agriculture persisted for many years, even as it became less relevant to people's daily lives. By the mid-20th century, however, the reasons for summer vacation had shifted somewhat. One factor was the rise of air conditioning, which made it more comfortable for people to work and live indoors during the hot summer months. Additionally, as more families began to take vacations and travel during the summer, schools adapted their schedules to accommodate these changes. Today, most schools in the United States still have a summer break of several weeks, typically lasting from late May or early June until late August or early September. Despite the origins of summer vacation in agriculture, some students today might argue that they would rather spend their summer months playing video games or lounging on the beach than working on a farm!

25. The iconic mortarboard hat worn during graduation ceremonies actually originated from the headgear worn by medieval scholars in Europe, called a biretta.

The biretta was a square-shaped cap with a tassel on top, typically made of black velvet or cloth. It was commonly worn by scholars and academics in medieval Europe, especially those in theology and law. The cap was often worn as a sign of distinction and achievement, indicating the wearer's level of education and expertise in their field. Over time, the design of the biretta evolved, with some versions having a curved peak or additional tassels. During the 14th century, the biretta began to be worn by students as well, particularly those studying at universities. The cap became a symbol of scholarly achievement and graduation, and was often worn during academic ceremonies and formal events. In the centuries that followed, the biretta continued to be an important symbol in academia, and was worn by students and scholars alike. In the late 19th and early 20th centuries, the design of the biretta began to change. The square shape was replaced by a more rounded cap, and the tassel was moved to the center of the cap. This new design was referred to as the "academic cap," and it became increasingly popular among universities and colleges in Europe and North America. Eventually, the academic cap evolved into the modern-day mortarboard, with its distinctive flat, square top and tassel hanging from the center. Today, the mortarboard is an iconic symbol of graduation and academic achievement, and is worn by students all over the world during commencement ceremonies and other formal events. And now, graduates can finally toss their caps in the air without fear of losing the tassel!

6. LITERATURE & LANGUAGE

26. The shortest story ever written is said to be "For sale: baby shoes, never worn," which is often attributed to Ernest Hemingway.

"For sale: baby shoes, never worn" is a six-word story that is often attributed to the American writer Ernest Hemingway. While the story's origins are unclear, it has become widely known and celebrated as an example of concise and powerful storytelling. Hemingway's authorship of the story is not definitively confirmed, but it is thought to have originated with him, based on anecdotal evidence from several sources. The story's power lies in its ability to evoke a sense of loss and tragedy with only a few words. By leaving out the details of the situation, the reader is left to imagine the circumstances that would lead to the sale of baby shoes that were never worn. The story has been analyzed and interpreted in many ways, with some seeing it as a commentary on the fleeting nature of life, and others as a statement on the futility of material possessions. While Hemingway's authorship of the story is uncertain, it is known that he was a master of concise and direct writing. He often used simple, declarative sentences and avoided elaborate descriptions or ornamentation in his writing. Hemingway's style of writing has had a significant influence on modern literature, and his work continues to be studied and admired by readers and writers alike. Anyhow, if the shoes had been worn, it would have been a different story altogether!

27. J.R.R. Tolkien typed the entire manuscript of "The Lord of the Rings" with two fingers.

J.R.R. Tolkien's "The Lord of the Rings" is one of the most beloved and widely read fantasy series of all time. The trilogy is an epic tale of adventure, magic, and the triumph of good over evil, and it has captivated readers for generations. What's even more impressive is that Tolkien typed the entire manuscript of this iconic work using just two fingers. Tolkien began writing "The Lord of the Rings" in the early 1940s, during World War II. He was working as an Oxford professor at the time, and he wrote much of the book in his spare time. Tolkien's typing style was notoriously slow, and he used a manual typewriter to compose his manuscript. Despite this, he was able to produce a massive work that spans over 1,000 pages. Tolkien's two-finger typing technique was not uncommon for writers of his time, as many people had not yet learned how to type properly. However, his dedication to the craft and his ability to produce such a complex and intricate work with just two fingers is a testament to his talent and perseverance as a writer. Today, "The Lord of the Rings" is considered a masterpiece of fantasy literature and has inspired countless works in the genre. It is remarkable to think that this epic tale was produced by an author typing with just two fingers, and it speaks to the power of dedication and hard work in the creative process. I guess we can all agree that Tolkien really gave two fingers to traditional typing methods!

28. J.K. Rowling, author of the Harry Potter series, was the first person to become a billionaire from writing books.

J.K. Rowling's rise to becoming a billionaire from writing books is a true rags-to-riches story. In the mid-1990s, Rowling was a struggling single mother living on government assistance in Edinburgh, Scotland. She wrote the first Harry Potter book in cafes while her baby slept in a stroller, and the manuscript was rejected by 12 publishers before it was finally accepted by Bloomsbury in 1996. The success of the first Harry Potter book was almost instantaneous, and it quickly became a bestseller. The subsequent books in the series were even more successful, with each one breaking sales records and receiving critical acclaim. The series has been translated into over 80 languages and has sold over 500 million copies worldwide. Rowling's success has not been without controversy, however. She has faced criticism for her portrayal of certain characters, particularly those from marginalized communities, and her political views have also been the subject of scrutiny. Nonetheless, there is no denying the impact that the Harry Potter series has had on popular culture and the publishing industry, and Rowling's success as an author has inspired countless aspiring writers around the world. Despite her massive success as an author, J.K. Rowling still hasn't received her Hogwarts acceptance letter!

29. The longest word in the English language has 189,819 letters and takes three and a half hours to pronounce. It is the chemical name for the largest known protein, Titin.

Titin is the largest known protein and is found in muscle tissue. The chemical name for Titin is technically a chemical formula, rather than a word, and is written as: METHIONYLTHREONYLTHREONYGLUTAMINYLARGINYL ISOLEUCINE. The name of this protein is often abbreviated to just "Titin" or "Ttn" for convenience. However, the full chemical name for the protein is incredibly long, consisting of 189,819 letters. To put that into perspective, the word "antidisestablishmentarianism", which is often cited as one of the longest words in the English language, has a mere 28 letters. The chemical name for Titin is so long because it describes the full sequence of amino acids that make up the protein. Amino acids are the building blocks of proteins, and the sequence in which they are arranged determines the function of the protein. In the case of Titin, the protein is responsible for providing elasticity and flexibility to muscle tissue. The chemical name for Titin is so long that it takes over three and a half hours to pronounce the entire word. However, it's worth noting that the full name is rarely used in scientific literature, and the protein is more commonly referred to by its shorter, abbreviated name. Despite its length, the chemical name for Titin is not officially recognized as the longest word in the English language, since it is a technical term rather than a word commonly used in everyday speech. So don't try to use it in a game of Scrabble!

30. Ernest Hemingway wrote standing up because he believed it helped him maintain his writing focus.

Ernest Hemingway, one of the most famous American writers of the 20th century, was known for his distinctive writing style, which often featured short sentences, simple language, and vivid descriptions. However, he was also known for his unique writing habits, such as writing standing up. Hemingway first began writing standing up while he was living in Paris in the 1920s. At the time, he was a struggling young writer, and he often wrote in small, cramped apartments with little space for a desk or writing table. He found that standing up at a high table allowed him to write more comfortably for longer periods of time, without getting too fatigued. But Hemingway's decision to write standing up was also based on his belief that it helped him maintain his writing focus. He once said, "When you sit down to write, write. Don't do anything else except go to the bathroom, and only do that if it absolutely can't be put off." By standing up, Hemingway felt he could stay more focused on his writing and avoid distractions. Hemingway's habit of writing standing up became legendary, and he continued to write this way for the rest of his life, even after he had become a successful and wealthy writer. Today, many writers and researchers believe that writing standing up can have benefits for creativity, productivity, and overall health, and some have even designed special standing desks and workstations to facilitate this writing posture. Who knew that the secret to great writing was just standing around?

7. TECHNOLOGY

31. The first computer programmer was a woman named Ada Lovelace who wrote the world's first machine algorithm for an early computing machine in the 1800s.

Ada Lovelace, born in 1815, was an English mathematician and writer who is credited with being the world's first computer programmer. She worked with Charles Babbage, a British mathematician and inventor who is considered to be the father of computers, on his proposed mechanical general-purpose computer, the Analytical Engine. In 1843, she translated an article on the Analytical Engine by Italian mathematician Luigi Menabrea into English. Her translation was accompanied by extensive notes —longer than Menabrea's original article— in which she described a method for using the Analytical Engine to calculate a sequence of numbers known as the Bernoulli numbers. These notes included an algorithm for calculating Bernoulli numbers, step-by-step instructions for programming the machine to carry out the calculation, and a description of how the machine would store and process data. Her pioneering work on the Analytical Engine is now considered the first computer program. In 1980, the U.S. Department of Defense honored her by naming a computer language, Ada, after her. Despite her groundbreaking work in computer programming, Ada Lovelace never got to experience the joys of a blue screen of death!

32.   The first-ever webcam was created in 1991 by a group of computer scientists at the University of Cambridge. It was used to monitor a coffee pot, allowing people to see if there was any coffee left before making the trip to refill it.

The first-ever webcam was created by a computer science team at the University of Cambridge in 1991, led by Dr. Quentin Stafford-Fraser and Dr. Paul Jardetzky. The team was trying to find a solution to a common problem they faced: the coffee pot in their department's break room was often empty when they arrived. The researchers decided to set up a camera pointed at the coffee pot and connected it to their local network so that anyone could check the camera feed from their computers. The camera used a video capture card and a custom software program to compress and transmit the video footage. The image was updated every three seconds and displayed on a web page that anyone on the network could access. The camera was named the "Trojan Room coffee pot" after the room where it was located, and it quickly became a popular tool for the researchers to check the coffee levels before making the trip to the break room. The webcam became famous outside of the University of Cambridge in 1993 when the World Wide Web was still in its early stages. A group of students at the University of Pennsylvania discovered the webcam and created a web page that linked to the coffee pot's live stream. The webcam continued to operate until the coffee pot was retired in 2001, and it is now on display at the Computer History Museum in Mountain View, California. And thus, the webcam revolutionized the way scientists procrastinated and avoided empty coffee pots!

33. The world's largest machine, the Large Hadron Collider, is a particle accelerator located in Switzerland and is used to study the fundamental nature of matter.

The Large Hadron Collider (LHC) is a remarkable feat of engineering and one of the most complex machines ever built by humans. It is a particle accelerator that is designed to recreate the conditions that existed just after the Big Bang. The LHC is located as deep as 175 meters underground and spans over 27 kilometers in circumference. It uses powerful magnets to accelerate two beams of subatomic particles, protons or lead ions, in opposite directions around the tunnel. When the beams reach close to the speed of light, they are made to collide at four points where the detectors are located. These collisions release enormous amounts of energy, allowing scientists to study the resulting subatomic particles, which can be extremely short-lived and difficult to detect. The data generated by these experiments can help scientists better understand the fundamental nature of matter, the origins of the universe, and even search for new particles like the Higgs Boson, which was discovered by the LHC in 2012. The LHC is a truly international project, involving thousands of scientists and engineers from around the world. It is operated by the European Organization for Nuclear Research (CERN) and has been in operation since 2008. Despite its enormous size and complexity, the LHC has proven to be an invaluable tool for scientific research and discovery. It's like a really expensive and high-tech version of smashing two toy cars together to see what pieces fly off!

34. **The first electric car was built in 1837 by Scottish inventor Robert Anderson. It was powered by non-rechargeable primary cells.**

Robert Anderson, a Scottish inventor, is credited with building the first electric car in 1837. Anderson's vehicle was powered by non-rechargeable primary cells, which were the early version of batteries. Anderson used a simple electric motor to propel the car forward, and the vehicle could reportedly travel up to 4 miles per hour. However, the car was not designed for practical use and was mainly a prototype to demonstrate the potential of electric power. Anderson's invention was an important step in the development of electric vehicles, but it was not until the late 19th century that electric cars began to gain popularity. In 1891, William Morrison of Des Moines, Iowa, built the first successful electric car in the United States, which could travel up to 14 miles per hour. Morrison's vehicle used a rechargeable battery, which made it more practical for everyday use. The early electric cars faced many challenges, including limited battery life, lack of charging infrastructure, and high production costs. As a result, the internal combustion engine quickly emerged as the dominant technology for powering vehicles, and electric cars fell out of favor for several decades. However, in recent years, electric cars have made a comeback as concerns over climate change and air pollution have increased. Unfortunately, Robert Anderson's electric car never caught on, as it was still slower than a horse-drawn carriage. But hey, at least he didn't have to worry about the horse leaving any surprises on the road!

35. The world's first website, which was published in 1991, is still live today. It was created by Sir Tim Berners-Lee, the inventor of the World Wide Web, and provided information about the project and how to access it.

The world's first website was created and published on August 6, 1991 by Sir Tim Berners-Lee while he was working at CERN, the European Organization for Nuclear Research. Berners-Lee developed the concept of the World Wide Web, a system of interlinked hypertext documents accessed via the Internet, in 1989. The first website, hosted on Berners-Lee's NeXT computer, was a simple page containing information about the World Wide Web project and how to access it. The website consisted of plain text and hyperlinks, which allowed users to navigate to other pages on the site. The site's address was "http://info.cern.ch/hypertext/WWW/TheProject.html", which is still live today, making it the oldest website still in existence. The site provided information about the World Wide Web, including its purpose, history, technical details, and future developments. The first website was a key milestone in the development of the World Wide Web, which has revolutionized the way people communicate, access information, and conduct business. Today, there are billions of websites on the Internet, covering a vast range of topics and services. The World Wide Web has become an essential part of modern life, and its impact on society and culture continues to grow. And to think, all this started with a single webpage and some hyperlinks. Talk about starting from the bottom, now we're here!

8. GEOGRAPHY

36. The lowest point on Earth is the Dead Sea, which is over 400 meters (1,300 feet) below sea level.

The Dead Sea is a saltwater lake located in the Jordan Rift Valley, bordered by Jordan to the east and Israel and Palestine to the west. It is known as the lowest point on Earth because its surface and shores lie more than 400 meters (1,300 feet) below sea level, making it the lowest point on the Earth's land surface. The Dead Sea is known for its high salt content, which is about 10 times saltier than regular seawater, and its mineral-rich mud. The high salt concentration makes it impossible for fish or other aquatic animals to live in the lake, hence the name "Dead" Sea. The high salinity also means that people can easily float on the water's surface without much effort. The Dead Sea's unique environment and its mineral-rich mud have made it a popular destination for tourists seeking health and wellness treatments. The mud is believed to have therapeutic properties, and many spas and resorts in the region offer treatments like mud baths and mineral-rich soaks. However, the Dead Sea is also facing environmental challenges. Its water level is dropping at an alarming rate due to diversion of the Jordan River, which feeds the lake, and increased water consumption in the surrounding areas. This has led to land subsidence, sinkholes, and other environmental problems. Conservation efforts are underway to try to save the Dead Sea and preserve its unique ecosystem. Despite its name, the Dead Sea is full of life... if you count all the tourists covered in mud!

37. The Great Barrier Reef, located off the coast of Australia, is the largest living structure on Earth and can be seen from space.

The Great Barrier Reef is an extraordinary natural wonder located in the Coral Sea, off the coast of Australia. It stretches over 2,300 kilometers (1430 miles) and covers an area of about 344,400 square kilometers, making it the world's largest coral reef system. The reef is composed of more than 2,900 individual coral reefs and 900 islands, as well as other organisms such as sponges, mollusks, and fish. The Great Barrier Reef is an extremely diverse ecosystem and is home to thousands of species, many of which are unique to the area. It is estimated that the reef is home to around 1,500 species of fish, 600 species of coral, and thousands of other marine creatures, including sharks, turtles, and whales. It is also an important breeding ground for many species of seabirds. But one of the most amazing things about the Great Barrier Reef is its sheer size. The reef is so large that it can be seen from space, making it one of the most recognizable landmarks on Earth. The Great Barrier Reef is also a popular destination for tourists, who come to explore the diverse marine life, go snorkeling or scuba diving, and visit the many islands that make up the reef. Despite its beauty, it is under threat from climate change, pollution, and other human activities. Rising sea temperatures are causing coral bleaching and the loss of marine life, while pollution from nearby cities and industries is damaging the reef's delicate ecosystem. Efforts are being made to protect the reef, including the creation of marine reserves and the reduction of carbon emissions. But did you know that the Great Barrier Reef has its own postcode? It's 4805!

38. The city of Istanbul is the only city in the world that is located in two continents, Europe and Asia, with the Bosphorus Strait separating the two.

The city of Istanbul, formerly known as Constantinople, is a major metropolis that straddles both Europe and Asia. It is situated on the Bosphorus Strait, a narrow waterway that connects the Black Sea with the Aegean Sea and separates Europe from Asia. The European side of Istanbul is home to many of the city's most famous landmarks, including the historic district of Sultanahmet, which contains iconic structures like the Hagia Sophia, the Blue Mosque, and the Topkapi Palace. The European side is also home to many modern neighborhoods, shopping centers, and business districts. On the Asian side of Istanbul, visitors can experience a different side of the city. The Asian side is less crowded and less touristy than the European side, but it is still full of life and culture. It is home to many parks and green spaces, as well as the trendy Kadikoy neighborhood, which is known for its restaurants, cafes, and nightlife. The Bosphorus Strait itself is a major attraction in Istanbul, with many ferries and boats offering tours and transportation between the two sides of the city. It is also a popular spot for fishing, swimming, and other water activities. Overall, Istanbul's unique location in both Europe and Asia makes it a fascinating destination for travelers who want to experience the best of both worlds. Whether you're interested in history, culture, cuisine, or just want to take in the stunning views, there is something for everyone in this vibrant city. And if you're lucky, you might even get to witness the infamous traffic jam caused by tourists trying to take selfies with both continents in the background!

39. The Lut Desert, located in Iran, is one of the hottest places on earth, with temperatures that can reach up to 70.7 degrees Celsius (159 degrees Fahrenheit).

The Lut Desert, also known as Dasht-e Lut, is a vast desert located in southeastern Iran. It is considered one of the driest and hottest places on Earth, and is known for its extreme temperatures and severe conditions. In fact, the Lut Desert is one of the hottest places on the planet, with temperatures that can reach up to 70.7 degrees Celsius (159 degrees Fahrenheit) during the day. The rugged environment of the Lut Desert has contributed to its unique geology and topography. The area is characterized by a mix of sand dunes, salt flats, and rocky terrain, and is home to a number of geological formations that are found nowhere else on Earth. These include large sand pyramids, deep canyons, and massive salt domes. Despite its extreme conditions, the Lut Desert is home to a number of unique plant and animal species that have adapted to survive in the harsh environment. These include desert foxes, sand cats, and several species of lizard and snake. The Lut Desert is also home to a number of important cultural and historical sites, including ancient trading routes and archaeological sites dating back thousands of years. In 2016, the Lut Desert was designated a UNESCO World Heritage site in recognition of its unique geology and cultural significance. However, the extreme conditions of the desert also make it a challenging and dangerous place to visit, and travelers are advised to take appropriate precautions when exploring the area. Just remember, if you're planning a trip to the Lut Desert, bring plenty of sunscreen, water, and maybe a frying pan and an egg to cook on the scorching hot sand!

40. There are currently two doubly landlocked countries and one doubly landlocked territory that is a de facto state.

A landlocked country is one that does not have direct access to the sea. However, there is an even rarer category of landlocked countries called doubly landlocked countries. These are countries that are not only landlocked, but also entirely surrounded by other landlocked countries. Currently, there are only two doubly landlocked countries in the world: Uzbekistan and Liechtenstein. In addition to these two countries, there is also one doubly landlocked territory that is a de facto state. This is the Nagorno-Karabakh Republic, a region in the South Caucasus that is internationally recognized as part of Azerbaijan, but is controlled by ethnic Armenian forces. The region is entirely surrounded by other landlocked countries, including Azerbaijan, Armenia, and Iran. Being doubly landlocked can pose significant challenges for these countries and territories, particularly when it comes to trade and transportation. Since they do not have access to the sea, they must rely on their neighboring countries to transport goods and resources in and out of their borders. This can make trade more expensive and less efficient, and can also create political tensions with neighboring countries. Despite these challenges, Uzbekistan and Liechtenstein have managed to develop relatively strong economies and maintain diplomatic relations with their neighbors. The Nagorno-Karabakh Republic, on the other hand, remains a highly contested and politically unstable region, with ongoing conflict between Armenia and Azerbaijan over its control. Despite being doubly landlocked, these countries still manage to keep their heads above water!

9. ANIMALS

41. a. A cat has the ability to rotate its ears 180 degrees, which helps it locate the source of a sound with incredible precision.
b. A dog's sense of smell is so powerful that it can detect odors up to 100,000 times better than a human.

a. Cats are well-known for their incredible hearing abilities, and their ears are designed to pick up sounds from all around them. What makes them so remarkable is that they can rotate their ears a full 180 degrees, which allows them to pinpoint the exact location of a sound with incredible precision. This ability comes in handy for hunting, as it enables them to locate prey with ease, even if it's hiding or moving quietly.
b. On the other hand, dogs are famous for their exceptional sense of smell. They have up to 300 million olfactory receptors in their noses, which is why they can detect scents that humans can't even imagine. In fact, their sense of smell is so powerful that they can detect odors up to 100,000 times better than humans. This ability is not just limited to identifying different scents, but they can also distinguish the faintest odor differences and track them over long distances. That's why dogs are used for a variety of tasks like tracking missing persons, detecting drugs, and sniffing out explosives.
It's safe to say that cats and dogs have some pretty impressive natural abilities; but let's be honest, their most impressive ability is still their talent for getting us humans to do whatever they want!

42. Sea otters hold hands while they sleep to prevent themselves from drifting apart.

Sea otters are known for their adorable appearance, playful behavior, and unique adaptations for life in the water. One such adaptation is their habit of holding hands while they sleep. This behavior, known as rafting, helps sea otters to stay together and avoid drifting apart while they rest. Sea otters are social animals that live in groups called rafts, which can consist of up to 100 individuals. By holding hands, sea otters can form a raft while they sleep, which provides them with a sense of security and helps to keep them warm in cold waters. Holding hands also helps to prevent sea otters from being carried away by strong currents or drifting out to sea. Sea otters are found along the coastlines of the northern Pacific Ocean, from California to Russia, and are considered a keystone species in their ecosystem. They play an important role in maintaining the health of kelp forests, which are critical habitats for many marine species. Despite their important ecological role, sea otters are considered an endangered species due to historical hunting and current threats from oil spills, pollution, and habitat loss. Sea otters may hold hands while they sleep, but they still manage to get more rest than most of us do!

43. Sloths have a slow digestive process and only defecate once a week to minimize their exposure to predators, losing up to 30% of their body weight in a single bowel movement.

Sloths are well-known for their slow-moving and leisurely nature, and this extends to their bathroom habits as well. Due to their low metabolic rate, sloths have a slow digestive process, which means they only defecate once every three to seven days. This behavior is actually an adaptation to their arboreal lifestyle, as sloths spend most of their time hanging upside down in trees. By defecating infrequently, they can minimize their exposure to predators on the ground, which include jaguars and eagles. When it comes time to defecate, sloths climb down from their trees and dig a small hole in the ground. They then assume a vulnerable position on the ground, where they are most exposed to predators. This behavior is risky, but necessary for the sloth's health, as a buildup of waste in their system can lead to serious health problems. Interestingly, when sloths defecate, they can lose up to 30% of their body weight in a single bowel movement. This is because the feces is made up of undigested plant matter, which can make up a significant portion of the sloth's body weight. Additionally, the defecation process can take up to a third of the sloth's day, as they are only able to produce small pellets at a time. Sloths are proof that you don't have to be quick on your feet to be number one in the bathroom!

44. African elephants can communicate with each other using infrasonic sounds that are too low for humans to hear.

African elephants are highly social animals and have complex communication systems that involve a variety of vocalizations, visual cues, and physical touch. In addition to audible sounds, they also use low-frequency, long-distance communication through infrasonic sounds. These sounds are produced by the contraction and relaxation of the elephant's vocal cords, which cause the air in their lungs to vibrate. The infrasonic calls of African elephants have a frequency range of 14-24 Hz, which is below the range of human hearing. Despite this, researchers have found that these calls can travel over great distances, up to several kilometers, through the air and even through the ground. African elephants use infrasonic calls to communicate with each other for a variety of reasons, such as warning of potential danger, identifying individuals, and finding potential mates. For example, a female elephant in estrus will produce infrasonic calls to attract potential mates from a distance. Male elephants can detect these calls from several kilometers away and will travel long distances to find the female. Overall, the use of infrasonic calls is a crucial aspect of the complex communication system of African elephants, allowing them to navigate their environment and social interactions in a highly effective manner. And just like that, elephants prove that communication is key in any successful relationship!

45. The fingerprints of koalas are so similar to those of humans that they have been confused at crime scenes.

The fingerprints of koalas and humans are indeed very similar. Like humans, koalas have distinctive fingerprints, which are unique to each individual. The fingerprints of koalas are formed in the same way as human fingerprints, through the pattern of ridges and grooves on their fingertips. The similarity between koala and human fingerprints has led to some confusion in the past, particularly in crime scenes where koalas have been present. In one instance, police in Australia were called to investigate a break-in at a veterinary clinic, where a koala had been found inside. The police officers took fingerprints from the scene, including from the door of the clinic, and were surprised to find a set of fingerprints that did not match any of their suspects. It turned out that the prints were from the koala, which had been curious and touched the door before leaving the clinic. The similarity between koala and human fingerprints has also led to some interesting research in the field of biomimicry, where scientists study natural systems to find inspiration for new technologies. Researchers have looked at the way that koalas use their fingerprints to grip onto trees, and have used this as a basis for designing new adhesives and materials for use in industry. Overall, the similarity between koala and human fingerprints highlights the fascinating and complex ways in which different species have evolved to adapt to their environments, and the potential for cross-species inspiration in fields such as technology and design. Who knew that koalas were so handy for both solving crimes and designing new adhesives?

10. SPORTS

46. The only sport to be played on the moon was golf, when Alan Shepard hit a ball in 1971.

On February 6, 1971, American astronaut Alan Shepard, who was part of the Apollo 14 mission, made history by hitting a golf ball on the moon. As the mission's commander, Shepard was also the fifth person to walk on the lunar surface, but he wanted to make his visit even more memorable. Shepard brought a golf club head, which he attached to a special tool that was designed to collect lunar soil samples. The tool was known as the "moon scoop," and Shepard used it as a makeshift golf club to hit two golf balls he had also brought with him. The first ball Shepard hit didn't go very far, as he swung one-handed because his spacesuit made it difficult to perform a full golf swing. However, the second ball he hit traveled much further and is estimated to have flown for over 200 yards due to the lower gravity on the moon. Although the feat of hitting a golf ball on the moon was a lighthearted moment in the otherwise serious business of space exploration, it helped to demonstrate the unique environment of the moon and the technological achievements of the Apollo program. We can probably finally say that golf is out of this world!

47. The oldest person to ever compete in the Olympic Games was Oscar Swahn of Sweden, who won a silver medal in shooting at the 1920 Olympics at the age of 72.

Oscar Swahn was a Swedish shooter who competed in six Olympic Games between 1908 and 1920. He won six medals in total, including three gold, two silver, and one bronze. At the 1920 Summer Olympics held in Antwerp, Belgium, he won his last Olympic medal, a silver, in the team running deer shooting event. He was 72 years old at the time, making him the oldest Olympic medalist in history. Swahn's shooting career spanned more than three decades, during which he won numerous national and international championships. He was known for his skill in the running deer shooting event, in which he would aim at a moving deer-shaped target. Swahn's Olympic achievements are even more remarkable considering the fact that he competed during a time when travel to the Olympic Games was arduous and expensive, and when there were no age restrictions for athletes. His longevity in the sport is a testament to his dedication and passion for shooting. I guess you could say Swahn was the original "silver fox" of the Olympic Games!

48. Basketball was invented by Canadian physical education instructor James Naismith in December 1891 as a way to keep his students active during the winter months.

Basketball is a sport that is enjoyed by millions of people around the world, but it has humble beginnings. James Naismith, a Canadian physical education instructor, was looking for a way to keep his students active during the winter months when outdoor sports were not possible. He was asked by his supervisor to come up with a new game that could be played indoors. Naismith began by writing out a set of rules for the new game, which he called "Basket Ball." The game was played in a gymnasium with two peach baskets placed on opposite ends of the court. The aim of the game was to throw a ball into the opposing team's basket while preventing them from doing the same. The first game of basketball was played on December 21, 1891, with nine players on each team. The game was a success, and Naismith's students enjoyed playing it. The first official basketball game was played in 1892, and by the early 1900s, the sport had gained popularity in colleges and universities across the United States. The rules of the game have evolved over time, but the basic principles of the sport remain the same. Today, basketball is played by millions of people around the world, from amateur pickup games to professional leagues like the NBA. Naismith's invention has become a beloved and popular sport, bringing people together and providing hours of entertainment and exercise. And to think, it all started with a peachy idea!

49. In 1967, Kathrine Switzer became the first woman to officially run the Boston Marathon.

Kathrine Switzer's participation in the Boston Marathon in 1967 was a groundbreaking moment in the history of women's sports. At the time, the Amateur Athletic Union (AAU) and the Boston Athletic Association (BAA), which organized the Boston Marathon, did not allow women to run in the race. Switzer, who was a student at Syracuse University at the time, had been training for the marathon and was determined to compete. To enter the race, Switzer registered under the name "K.V. Switzer" and was assigned bib number 261. She started the race along with her coach and her boyfriend, but around mile two, a race official noticed that she was a woman and tried to physically remove her from the course. Switzer's boyfriend, who was running with her, pushed the official away and Switzer continued to run. Despite the harassment and intimidation she faced during the race, Switzer completed the 26.2-mile course in four hours and twenty minutes. Her participation in the race received widespread media coverage and brought attention to the issue of gender discrimination in sports. Switzer went on to become a pioneer for women's running and helped to pave the way for other women to compete in marathons and other endurance events. In 1972, the Boston Marathon officially began allowing women to enter the race, and Switzer went on to compete in the race several more times throughout her career. After the incident, the race official was probably regretting his decision to mess with Switzer, as she went on to show the world what women are capable of accomplishing!

50. The sport of parkour originated in France in the 1980s and involves using acrobatic movements to navigate through obstacles and urban environments.

Parkour is a discipline that involves moving through the environment in the most efficient way possible, using only the human body and the surrounding structures as tools. Parkour athletes, known as traceurs, focus on speed, agility, balance, and strength to move quickly and fluidly through any obstacle in their path. The sport was created in the commune of Lisses in the 1980s, where it was initially called "Art du Deplacement" ("Art of Movement"). The founder of parkour is considered to be David Belle, who was inspired by his father's military training and his own experiences growing up in an urban environment. Belle, along with other early practitioners, developed the discipline as a way to train their bodies and minds for survival in any situation. Parkour has since grown into an international sport and cultural phenomenon, with its own competitions, training facilities, and community. The sport has inspired movies, video games, and TV shows, and is now recognized as an official sport in many countries. Traceurs continue to push the limits of what is possible with their incredible athleticism, creativity, and fearlessness in the face of seemingly impossible obstacles. Who needs a gym membership when you can just climb buildings?

11. FOOD & BEVERAGE

51. The world's spiciest pepper is so hot it can cause hallucinations.

The Carolina Reaper pepper was created in 2013 by a farmer named Ed Currie in South Carolina, USA. It was bred through a combination of different pepper varieties to create an incredibly spicy pepper that was hotter than any other pepper at the time. The pepper's spiciness is measured on the Scoville scale, which is a measure of the concentration of capsaicin, the chemical that causes the burning sensation in hot peppers. The Carolina Reaper has an average Scoville rating of over 1.5 million units, which is more than twice as hot as the previous record holder, the Trinidad Moruga Scorpion pepper. The intense heat of the Carolina Reaper can cause a range of physical reactions, including intense pain and sweating, as well as more extreme reactions such as hallucinations and vomiting in some cases. The sensation of eating a Carolina Reaper is often described as feeling like your mouth is on fire, with the heat building to a peak and then slowly subsiding over several minutes. Despite the extreme heat of the Carolina Reaper, it has gained popularity among some spicy food enthusiasts who enjoy the challenge of eating the world's spiciest pepper. There are even competitions where people compete to see who can eat the most Carolina Reapers in a set amount of time. Just remember, if you decide to try the Carolina Reaper, keep a glass of milk and a fire extinguisher nearby!

52. Champagne can only be called "Champagne" if it is produced in the Champagne region of France and follows specific production methods.

Champagne is a sparkling wine that is known for its bubbly effervescence and is often associated with celebrations and special occasions. The Champagne region of France, which is located northeast of Paris, has been producing this unique wine since the 17th century. The region's soil and climate are well-suited to growing the specific grape varieties used in Champagne production, which include Chardonnay, Pinot Noir, and Pinot Meunier. In order to be called "Champagne," the wine must be produced in accordance with specific rules and regulations established by the French government. These regulations cover every aspect of Champagne production, from the type of grapes used to the fermentation and aging process. For example, Champagne must be made using a process called "méthode champenoise," which involves a secondary fermentation in the bottle to create the wine's signature bubbles. The use of the term "Champagne" is also protected by international law through several agreements, including the Madrid Agreement, the Lisbon Agreement, and the World Trade Organization's Agreement on Trade-Related Aspects of Intellectual Property Rights (TRIPS). This means that only wines produced in the Champagne region of France and following the specific production methods can legally be labeled as "Champagne." Wines made using the same methods outside of the region are typically referred to as "sparkling wines". So remember, if you're ever in France and someone offers you "Champagne" that was made outside of the Champagne region, you're legally allowed to say "non, merci!"

53. The first chocolate bar was created in 1847 by British chocolatier Joseph Fry.

The creation of the first chocolate bar by Joseph Fry in 1847 marked a significant milestone in the history of chocolate. Prior to the invention of the chocolate bar, chocolate was mainly consumed in the form of a beverage, as it was too brittle to be molded into a solid form. However, Fry's innovation in mixing cocoa powder with cocoa butter and sugar resulted in a smooth and solid chocolate that could be easily molded and packaged. The first chocolate bars were made by hand and were very expensive, as the process of making them was labor-intensive. However, the industrial revolution brought about significant changes in the production of chocolate, making it more accessible to the general population. The introduction of mechanized processes for grinding cocoa beans, tempering chocolate, and molding bars allowed for large-scale production and a decrease in the cost of chocolate. The popularity of chocolate bars grew rapidly, and by the early 20th century, they had become a staple of many people's diets. Today, chocolate bars come in a wide variety of flavors and styles, with some containing nuts, fruit, or other types of candy. They are enjoyed by millions of people around the world and have become an integral part of many cultures. It's safe to say that Joseph Fry's creation of the chocolate bar was a sweet success!

54. Honey never spoils. Archaeologists have found pots of honey in ancient Egyptian tombs that are still edible after thousands of years.

Honey is one of the few foods that never spoils, thanks to its unique chemical composition and the fact that it is naturally antimicrobial. Honey is primarily made up of sugars, such as fructose and glucose, which are hygroscopic, meaning they contain very little water. The low water content of honey makes it inhospitable to the growth of bacteria and other microorganisms, which would otherwise cause it to spoil. In addition to its low water content, honey also contains small amounts of hydrogen peroxide, which is a natural antimicrobial agent that helps to kill off bacteria and other pathogens. When bees collect nectar from flowers, they add an enzyme called glucose oxidase, which produces hydrogen peroxide when the honey is exposed to moisture. Because of its long shelf life, honey has been a staple food for humans for thousands of years, and has been used as a natural sweetener, medicine, and preservative. In ancient Egypt, honey was often used to embalm mummies, and pots of honey have been found in tombs that are still perfectly edible after thousands of years. Despite its many health benefits, it is important to note that honey should not be given to infants under the age of one, as it may contain spores of the bacteria that causes botulism, which can be deadly to young children. If you ever find a jar of honey that has gone bad, it's probably a honey impostor trying to pull the wool over your eyes. Don't fall for their sticky, deceitful ways!

55.   The world's most expensive coffee is called Kopi Luwak, which is made from coffee beans that have been eaten and excreted by the Asian palm civet, and can cost up to $100 per kilogram for farmed beans and $1,300 per kilogram for wild-collected beans.

Kopi Luwak, also known as civet coffee, is produced by collecting the droppings of the Asian palm civet, a small mammal native to Southeast Asia. The civet eats the ripest coffee cherries, but the digestive enzymes in its stomach break down the fruit, leaving the coffee beans intact. After the beans are excreted, they are collected, cleaned, and roasted to make coffee. The production of Kopi Luwak has become controversial in recent years due to concerns over animal welfare. Some producers have resorted to keeping civets in small cages and force-feeding them coffee cherries to increase production, leading to animal cruelty and poor-quality coffee. Despite its high cost, the taste of Kopi Luwak is not universally praised. Some coffee connoisseurs have criticized it for its lack of complexity and notes of fecal matter. However, the high price of Kopi Luwak has made it a status symbol among some consumers, leading to concerns over counterfeit coffee being sold as authentic Kopi Luwak. To combat this, some producers have implemented certification processes to ensure the authenticity and ethical production of the coffee. So, if you want a cup of Kopi Luwak, just make sure it's the real deal and not a crappy imitation!

12. ART

56. The color blue was once the most expensive pigment to use in art, as it was made from lapis lazuli, a rare and expensive stone found in Afghanistan.

For thousands of years, the blue color was considered one of the most precious and expensive colors in the world of art. Lapis lazuli, a semi-precious stone found in the mountains of Afghanistan, was the primary source of blue pigment for centuries. The stone was mined by hand, transported across treacherous terrain, and then ground into a fine powder to be used as paint. Due to the difficulty of acquiring and processing the stone, the color blue was reserved for only the most important figures and artworks, such as religious paintings, frescoes, and royal portraits. The use of lapis lazuli as a pigment dates back to ancient times, with the stone being used by the Egyptians, Greeks, and Romans. In medieval Europe, the pigment was highly valued and often reserved for use in illuminated manuscripts and religious paintings. During the Renaissance, artists such as Michelangelo and Raphael used the pigment to add depth and richness to their works, and it became a symbol of prestige and power. With the advent of modern technology, synthetic blue pigments were developed, making blue more accessible and affordable for artists. However, lapis lazuli is still used by some artists today for its unique and vibrant qualities. And if you happen to have a painting with a lot of blue in it, you can proudly say that you own a piece of the world's most expensive color!

57. The first recorded graffiti art is believed to be the prehistoric cave paintings in Lascaux, France, which date back to around 15,000 BCE.

The Lascaux cave paintings, located in southwestern France, were discovered in 1940 by a group of young boys who stumbled upon the entrance while playing in the woods. The cave contains some of the finest examples of Paleolithic art, with over 600 paintings and engravings depicting animals, humans, and abstract symbols. The artists used mineral pigments, charcoal, and other materials to create the images, which are believed to have been created between 15,000 and 17,000 years ago. The Lascaux cave paintings are a significant example of early human art, showcasing the importance of visual expression in human culture. The paintings offer insights into the beliefs, values, and daily lives of our prehistoric ancestors, as well as their artistic abilities and creativity. Today, the Lascaux cave is closed to the public in an effort to preserve the fragile artwork, but a replica cave, known as Lascaux II, has been constructed nearby and is open for visitors to experience the awe-inspiring artistry of our distant past. Fun fact: The Lascaux cave paintings were so impressive that even Pablo Picasso himself visited the cave and remarked, "We have learned nothing in twelve thousand years"!

58. The art of paper folding, or origami, originated in Japan in the 17th century and has since become a popular art form worldwide.

Origami is the Japanese art of paper folding, which involves folding a single sheet of paper into a three-dimensional object, without cutting or gluing the paper. The word "origami" comes from the Japanese words "ori," meaning "folding," and "kami," meaning "paper." Origami was initially used for religious purposes, such as making offerings to the gods or as ceremonial decorations. It was later popularized among the samurai class in Japan, who used it to create elaborate designs, including animals and flowers. In the 19th century, origami became more widely known in Japan and began to spread to other parts of the world. Today, origami is practiced by people of all ages and backgrounds, and has become a popular art form in many countries, with many artists creating intricate designs and sculptures using just a single sheet of paper. There are even international origami competitions held annually, where artists showcase their skills and compete for prizes. And if you ever need to wrap a gift, just fold a piece of paper into a crane and call it a day!

59. The world's oldest surviving music instrument is the Divje Babe flute, a carved bone flute discovered in a Slovenian cave, dating back to around 43,000 years ago.

The Divje Babe flute is a unique and fascinating artifact that offers valuable insights into the history of human music-making. It was discovered in 1995 by archaeologist Ivan Turk in the Divje Babe archaeological park in northwestern Slovenia. The flute is made of a hollowed bear femur bone, and has four finger holes and a V-shaped mouthpiece. The bone also contains several notches and holes that suggest it may have been intentionally modified to create different pitches. The discovery of the Divje Babe flute challenges the widely-held belief that music-making emerged only around 40,000 years ago, during the Upper Paleolithic period. It suggests that early humans had the capacity for musical expression much earlier than previously thought. The flute's design and playability have been studied extensively by archaeologists and musicians, and have even been recreated by modern-day flute makers. Despite its age, the Divje Babe flute's authenticity has been the subject of debate among scholars. Some experts argue that the notches on the bone were made by natural causes rather than human modification, and that the "flute" was actually just a chewed-up bone. However, most researchers agree that the bone's intentional modifications and musical characteristics are strong evidence of its use as a musical instrument. So, if you ever see a bear with a femur bone flute, just know that it's following a very ancient tradition!

60. The first photograph ever taken, called "View from the Window at Le Gras," was captured by Joseph Nicéphore Niépce in 1826. It took 8 hours of exposure time to create the image.

"View from the Window at Le Gras" is not only the first photograph ever taken, but it is also the oldest surviving camera photograph in the world. The photograph was taken using a process called heliography, which involved coating a pewter plate with bitumen and then exposing it to light through a camera obscura. The bitumen hardened where it was exposed to light, creating a permanent image. The photograph shows the view from Niépce's window at his estate in Burgundy, France. The image is a primitive black and white landscape with a faint view of trees, rooftops, and the sky. Due to the long exposure time, the image appears somewhat blurry, and the shadows are reversed, as if viewed through a negative. After Niépce's death, his son sold the rights to his photographic process to Louis Daguerre, who improved upon the technique and went on to create the daguerreotype, a type of photograph that was much more detailed and required a much shorter exposure time. Nonetheless, Niépce's work was a groundbreaking achievement in the history of photography and paved the way for the development of modern photography. I guess you could say that Niépce's photograph was the original "slow shutter" art!

13. MUSIC

61. Beethoven composed his famous Ninth Symphony while completely deaf, relying on vibrations he could feel through the floorboards to create the music.

Ludwig van Beethoven, one of the greatest composers in the history of classical music, began to lose his hearing in his late twenties and was almost completely deaf by the time he composed his Ninth Symphony. Despite this, he continued to compose and conduct music, relying on his memory of the sounds he had previously heard and feeling the vibrations of the music through the floorboards. When Beethoven composed his Ninth Symphony, he had not performed in public for over a decade, and his deafness was a major obstacle in its composition. He was no longer able to hear the music he was writing, and instead had to rely on the visual and tactile elements of the score. He would place his ear on the piano and feel the vibrations of the notes to get a sense of how they sounded. Despite these challenges, Beethoven was able to create a masterpiece that has been celebrated for centuries. The Ninth Symphony is known for its dramatic use of chorus and soloists in the final movement, which includes the famous "Ode to Joy" melody. Despite losing his hearing, Beethoven continued to compose and create beautiful music, proving that the saying "if you can't hear the music, feel the music" is not just a cheesy line from a rom-com!

62. The song "Happy Birthday" is copyrighted and brings in an estimated $2 million in royalties each year.

The song, which is often sung to celebrate birthdays, was written by Mildred and Patty Hill in 1893 under the title "Good Morning to All." The tune and lyrics were originally intended as a simple classroom greeting for young children. In 1935, the Hill sisters' song was adapted into "Happy Birthday to You" by a group of musicians who were performing a play. The song quickly gained popularity and became a staple at birthday parties and other celebrations around the world. However, the song's copyright was acquired by Warner/Chappell Music in 1988, and the company began enforcing its ownership by charging licensing fees for public performances of the song. As a result, the use of "Happy Birthday" in films, television shows, and public performances has been restricted and subject to fees. Many people have criticized the copyright as an example of overreaching intellectual property law and have called for the song to be placed in the public domain. In 2015, a federal judge ruled that Warner/Chappell Music did not hold a valid copyright to the song, and it has since been free to use without fear of infringement claims. Nonetheless, the song's complex legal history and continued association with commercial interests have made it a unique and intriguing piece of music trivia. Just remember, if you sing "Happy Birthday" in public, make sure you have a lawyer on standby!

63. The term "rock and roll" was originally a slang term for sex in African American music before it became associated with the genre of music we know today.

The term "rock and roll" has a long and complicated history, with its origins dating back to African American culture in the early 20th century. In the early 1920s, the term "rocking" or "rocking and rolling" was used in blues music to refer to sexual activity. This slang term for sex was then picked up by various African American musicians and incorporated into their music. For example, in the 1934 song "Rockin' and Rollin'" by Lil Johnson, the lyrics include: "I'm gonna rock and roll with my baby all night long." The song's title and lyrics make it clear that "rocking and rolling" is a euphemism for sexual activity. As African American music styles like blues and R&B evolved in the 1940s and 1950s, the term "rock and roll" began to be used more broadly to refer to the music itself. It's unclear exactly when and how this shift in meaning occurred, but it's possible that it was due to the increasing popularity of these genres of music among white audiences. By the mid-1950s, "rock and roll" had become a distinct genre of music with its own style, sound, and cultural significance. However, the roots of the term in African American culture and its original connotations of sexual activity are important to remember when considering the history of the genre. Despite the term "rock and roll" originating as a euphemism for sex, it's safe to say that most people today associate it more with head-banging than bed-banging!

64. The shortest song ever recorded is "You Suffer" by the British band Napalm Death. The song is only 1.316 seconds long and contains the lyrics "You suffer, but why?"

Napalm Death is a British grindcore band known for their extreme music style and political lyrics. In 1987, the band released their debut album "Scum" which features the shortest song ever recorded, "You Suffer." The song is only 1.316 seconds long and consists of the repeated lyrics "You suffer, but why?" screamed over a blast of distorted guitars and drums. Despite its brevity, "You Suffer" has become a cult classic among fans of extreme music and has even been featured in video games, commercials, and films. The song's status as the shortest song ever recorded has also made it a topic of interest for music trivia enthusiasts and Guinness World Records. The origins of the song's lyrics are somewhat obscure, with some fans speculating that they are a reference to the Buddhist concept of suffering or a commentary on the futility of human existence. Regardless of its meaning, "You Suffer" has become a unique piece of music history and a testament to the power of brevity and intensity in art. It just goes to show that sometimes less is more, especially when it comes to screaming about suffering over a wall of noise!

65. **a. Amirhossein Molaei holds the Guinness Book of Records title for the highest vocal note produced by a man (F#8, 5989 Hz).**

b. The lowest note ever sung by a human was achieved by American singer Tim Storms. He hit a note with a frequency of 0.189 Hz.

a. Amirhossein Molaei is a vocalist from Iran who, in 2019, achieved an extraordinary feat in the field of music: he holds the Guinness Book of Records title for the highest vocal note produced by a man, an impressive F#8 with a frequency of 5989 Hz. To put this into perspective, F#8 is three octaves and one note higher than the highest note on a standard piano keyboard, which has a frequency of 4186 Hz. The ability to hit such an incredibly high note is a testament to Molaei's exceptional vocal range and control. Singers who can hit notes in this range are often referred to as "sopranissimos," a term that denotes a voice type that is higher than a soprano. In fact, the term "sopranissimo" is so rare that it's not even included in most standard dictionaries.

b. The lowest note ever sung by a human was achieved by American singer Tim Storms. He hit a note with a frequency of 0.189 Hz, which is roughly eight octaves below the lowest G on a piano. This note is so low that it is below the threshold of human hearing and can only be detected by specialized equipment. Tim Storms has a vocal range of 10 octaves and is able to hit notes that are incredibly low. Singers like Tim Storms are often referred to as bassos profundos, a term that denotes a voice type that is lower than a bass. It's safe to say that both Amirhossein Molaei and Tim Storms have reached new lows and highs in the singing world!

14. PSYCHOLOGY

66. The "bystander effect" is a social phenomenon in which people are less likely to intervene in an emergency situation when there are more people around.

The bystander effect is a social psychological phenomenon that refers to the tendency of people to not offer help or intervene in emergency situations when there are other people present. The concept was first introduced by psychologists Bibb Latané and John Darley in 1968 following the infamous murder of Kitty Genovese in New York City in 1964. The case received widespread media coverage, as it was reported that many people had witnessed the murder or heard Genovese's screams, but none of them intervened or called the police. Since then, numerous studies have been conducted to explore the bystander effect and its underlying causes. One possible explanation is diffusion of responsibility, where people feel less personally responsible to take action when there are others around who could also help. Additionally, social influence and conformity can play a role, as people may look to others to determine what the appropriate response to a situation is. Fear of social disapproval or negative consequences for intervening can also discourage people from taking action. The bystander effect has important implications for emergency situations, such as accidents, violence, or medical emergencies, as the presence of multiple bystanders can reduce the likelihood of someone receiving timely assistance. So next time you're in an emergency situation and need help, remember: it's better to have one reliable friend than a dozen hesitant bystanders!

**67.   According to the psychological theory of cognitive disso-
nance, people tend to experience discomfort when their beliefs or attitudes are inconsistent with their behavior, leading
them to modify either their beliefs or their behavior to reduce
the dissonance.**

Cognitive dissonance is a psychological theory developed by
Leon Festinger in the 1950s. It refers to the mental discomfort
or psychological stress that arises from holding two or more
conflicting beliefs, values, or ideas at the same time. Cognitive
dissonance is a common experience in daily life, as people often encounter situations where their beliefs and behaviors are
inconsistent. The theory suggests that when a person experiences cognitive dissonance, they will be motivated to reduce
the discomfort by changing their behavior, their beliefs, or
their attitudes. For example, imagine that a person who values
environmental sustainability takes a job at a company that
engages in environmentally damaging practices. This person
may experience cognitive dissonance, as their values and behaviors are in conflict. To reduce the discomfort, they may
either change their behavior by finding a new job or change
their beliefs by justifying their decision to work at the company. Cognitive dissonance can also occur when people encounter information that conflicts with their existing beliefs or attitudes. For example, if someone believes that smoking is not
harmful to health and then comes across scientific evidence to
the contrary, they may experience cognitive dissonance. To
reduce the discomfort, they may either change their beliefs by
accepting the new information or change their behavior by
quitting smoking. So cognitive dissonance is like wearing two
left shoes, but for your brain!

68. People tend to overestimate how much others notice their mistakes or flaws, a phenomenon known as the "spotlight effect".

The "spotlight effect" is a term used to describe the phenomenon where individuals overestimate how much attention others are paying to their appearance or behavior. This tendency to believe that we are the center of attention is often due to a self-focused bias, which causes individuals to prioritize their own experiences and perceptions over those of others. Research on the spotlight effect has shown that people tend to believe that their mistakes or flaws are more noticeable to others than they actually are. For example, one study asked participants to wear a t-shirt with a picture of Barry Manilow on it and then estimate how many people noticed the shirt. Participants tended to overestimate the number of people who noticed the shirt by a wide margin. Another study asked participants to wear an embarrassing t-shirt and then walk into a room full of strangers. The participants believed that the strangers would judge them harshly for the shirt, but in reality, the strangers paid very little attention to the shirt and the participants were not judged negatively. The spotlight effect can lead to self-consciousness, anxiety, and a reluctance to take risks or try new things. However, understanding that other people are likely not paying as much attention to us as we think can help to reduce these negative effects and allow us to feel more confident in ourselves and our actions. Remember, the spotlight effect is like the moon - just because it's out doesn't mean everyone's staring at it!

69. People who experience déjà vu may actually have a better memory than those who don't, as it is thought to occur when the brain is briefly "confused" and processes current experiences as memories.

Déjà vu is a common phenomenon that occurs when someone feels like they have experienced the current situation before, even though they know that it is not possible. While it can be a strange and disorienting experience, it is generally harmless and lasts only a few seconds. There are several theories about why déjà vu occurs, and one of them suggests that it may be linked to memory. According to this theory, déjà vu happens when the brain processes current experiences as memories, rather than as new experiences. This could be because the brain is working too quickly, and the information is processed by the wrong part of the brain. Research has shown that people who experience déjà vu may actually have a better memory than those who don't. In a study published in the journal Memory and Cognition, researchers found that people who reported experiencing déjà vu scored higher on memory tests than those who did not. This suggests that déjà vu may be a sign of a well-functioning memory system. It's worth noting, however, that not all researchers agree with this theory, and there may be other factors that contribute to déjà vu. For example, some studies suggest that déjà vu may be linked to temporal lobe epilepsy, while others suggest that it may be a result of anxiety or stress. Regardless of the cause, déjà vu is a reminder that there is still much we don't know about the workings of the human brain and the mysteries of consciousness, and that it's not a glitch in the Matrix, but rather a quirk in our brain's software!

70. The "Hawthorne effect" is the phenomenon in which people change their behavior when they know they are being observed.

The Hawthorne effect is named after a series of studies conducted in the 1920s and 1930s at the Hawthorne Works, a factory near Chicago, Illinois. The studies were designed to investigate the relationship between lighting conditions and worker productivity. However, the researchers found that productivity increased regardless of whether the lighting was improved or worsened. They concluded that the mere fact of being observed and receiving attention from researchers had a positive effect on worker productivity. The Hawthorne effect has since been observed in a wide range of settings, including education, healthcare, and research. For example, students may perform better on exams when they know they are being observed by their teachers, or patients may exhibit better health outcomes when they know they are participating in a clinical trial. The effect can also occur in non-research settings, such as when people change their behavior in response to social media attention or public scrutiny. The Hawthorne effect can be seen as a type of self-fulfilling prophecy, in which people's expectations of being observed or receiving attention lead them to change their behavior in the desired direction. The effect is also related to the idea of social facilitation, which suggests that people perform better on simple tasks when they are being watched, but worse on more complex tasks. Just remember, if you're ever feeling unproductive, all you need is someone to watch you and give you some attention!

15. HEALTH

71. The human body contains more bacteria than human cells, with over 100 trillion bacteria living on the human body.

It may come as a surprise, but the human body contains more bacterial cells than human cells. The number of bacterial cells in and on the human body is estimated to be around 100 trillion, while the number of human cells is estimated to be around 30 trillion. This means that the ratio of bacteria to human cells is roughly 3:1. The majority of these bacteria are found in the gut, where they play a crucial role in digestion, immune system regulation, and the synthesis of vitamins and other important compounds. In fact, the gut microbiome, which refers to the community of bacteria living in the gut, is often referred to as the "forgotten organ" due to its important functions. However, not all bacteria in the body are beneficial. Some species can cause infections and disease if they overgrow or penetrate the body's natural defenses. The balance between beneficial and harmful bacteria is essential for maintaining good health. Scientists are investigating how changes in the microbiome can contribute to various health conditions, such as obesity, diabetes, and autoimmune diseases, and are exploring ways to manipulate the microbiome to improve health outcomes. So, the next time someone says you're full of bacteria, you can take it as a compliment!

72. A small percentage of people experience a rare condition called "exploding head syndrome," in which they hear loud, sudden noises that sound like explosions or gunshots while falling asleep or waking up.

Exploding Head Syndrome (EHS) is a rare and relatively unknown sleep disorder that is characterized by loud and sudden noises that occur during the transition between sleep stages. The noises are usually described as sounding like explosions, gunshots, or even thunderclaps. These sounds are not real, but are perceived as being very loud and sudden, which can cause a great deal of distress and anxiety. EHS episodes typically occur during the transition from wakefulness to sleep, or from one stage of sleep to another. They can be accompanied by a number of physical symptoms, such as a racing heart, sweating, and a feeling of pressure in the head or ears. Although the exact cause of EHS is unknown, it is believed to be related to the misfiring of neurons in the brainstem that control the muscles involved in hearing. This misfiring can cause the perception of loud sounds even when no actual noise is present. EHS is a relatively rare condition, it is more common in women than men, and tends to occur more frequently in people who are over 50 years of age. Treatment for EHS usually involves reassurance and education about the condition, as well as strategies to help manage the anxiety and distress that it can cause. In some cases, medications such as antidepressants or anticonvulsants may be prescribed to help reduce the frequency and severity of EHS episodes. So, if you think your neighbor's fireworks show is loud, wait until you experience EHS!

73. Your brain can actually experience "phantom vibration syndrome," where you think your phone is vibrating in your pocket, even when it's not.

"Phantom vibration syndrome" or "phantom ringing syndrome" is a phenomenon where people perceive a false sensation of vibration or ringing in their phone, even when it is not vibrating or ringing. This feeling is often described as a "tingling" or "buzzing" sensation in the pocket or belt where the phone is carried. The exact cause of phantom vibration syndrome is not known, but it is believed to be related to the way our brains interpret sensory information. The constant exposure to vibrations and sounds from phones can create a conditioning effect on our brains, leading them to expect these sensations even when they are not present. Phantom vibration syndrome is a common experience, with studies showing that up to 80% of people have experienced it at some point. It is particularly common among heavy phone users, such as those who use their phones for work or social media. While phantom vibration syndrome is generally harmless, it can be a sign of a larger problem if it is accompanied by other symptoms such as hearing voices or seeing things that aren't there. If you experience these symptoms, it is important to talk to a healthcare provider to rule out any underlying medical conditions. Remember, if you feel your phone vibrating but it's not actually ringing, it's probably not a sign that you're popular. Sorry to break it to you!

74. Sneezes can release up to 40,000 droplets into the air, potentially spreading viruses and bacteria, and generate plumes of up to 8 meters (26 ft).

When we sneeze, we don't just expel air, but we also release droplets that contain a mix of saliva, mucus, and other particles from our respiratory system. These droplets can vary in size, and the smaller ones can remain suspended in the air for a longer period of time, increasing the risk of transmission. This release of air can also create a cloud of droplets that can quickly travel long distances, potentially infecting others nearby. Studies have shown that larger droplets tend to fall to the ground more quickly, while smaller ones can remain suspended in the air for longer periods of time, increasing the risk of transmission. To prevent the spread of infectious diseases, public health organizations have recommended a variety of measures to minimize the risk of transmission. In addition to covering the mouth and nose when sneezing or coughing, people are advised to wash their hands frequently and avoid close contact with individuals who are sick. It's also worth noting that sneezing is not always a sign of illness, as it can also be triggered by non-infectious irritants such as pollen, dust, or pepper. However, in the context of a contagious disease, it's important to take precautions to minimize the risk of transmitting the virus or bacteria to others. As it turns out, "bless you" is more than just a polite response to a sneeze - it might be the only thing preventing a cloud of droplets from infecting everyone around you. So remember, next time you sneeze, cover up and say your blessings!

75. The longest recorded time without sleep is 11 days, set by a high school student in 1964.

The idea of staying up for a long time may sound appealing to some people, but it can have serious negative effects on the body and mind. The current world record for the longest recorded time without sleep is held by Randy Gardner, a 17-year-old high school student from San Diego, California. Gardner set the record in 1964, after staying awake for a total of 264.4 hours, or 11 days and 24 minutes. During his ordeal, Gardner experienced a range of symptoms, including hallucinations, blurred vision, slurred speech, memory and concentration problems, and mood swings. He also had difficulty with motor coordination and reaction times. Despite these symptoms, Gardner was able to function fairly normally, even playing basketball and driving a car during the later stages of his sleep deprivation. It is not recommended for anyone to attempt to break Gardner's record or stay awake for such an extended period of time. Sleep is a vital biological function that is necessary for our physical and mental health, and prolonged sleep deprivation can lead to serious health problems, including cognitive impairment, depression, and even death. It's important to prioritize getting enough sleep every night to maintain optimal health and well-being. Remember, the only time it's appropriate to stay up for 11 days straight is during a binge-watching. Otherwise, get some sleep!

16. FASHION

76. The high heel shoe was actually originally designed for men, not women. It was first worn by Persian horse riders in the 9th century to help them keep their feet in stirrups.

The high heel shoe, a popular fashion accessory worn mainly by women, has an interesting history dating back to the 9th century. Although today, high heels are seen as a symbol of femininity, they were initially designed for men. In fact, the first people to wear high heels were Persian horse riders, who wore them to help them keep their feet in stirrups while riding. Over time, high heels became popular among European aristocrats, particularly in the 16th century. Men wore them as a symbol of their status and wealth, as the height of the heel was an indication of their social standing. However, as fashion changed over time, men's high heels eventually fell out of favor, and the design became more commonly associated with women's fashion. In the 19th century, high heels became a staple of women's fashion, particularly in Europe and North America. The height of the heel varied over time, from small kitten heels in the 1950s to the towering platform shoes of the 1970s. While men's high heels are not as common as they once were, some designers and fashion-forward individuals have revived the trend in recent years. Who says you can't have your high heel and wear it too?

77. The most expensive watch ever sold at auction is the Patek Philippe Grandmaster Chime Ref. 6300A-010, which was auctioned by Christie's in 2019 for a staggering $31 million.

This unique timepiece was created specifically for the auction to celebrate Patek Philippe's 175th anniversary, and it was the only one of its kind ever made. The watch has 20 complications, including five chiming modes, two of which are patented world firsts. It has a striking blue enamel dial with white gold hands and hour markers, and it comes with two interchangeable dials in rose gold and white gold. The case is made of stainless steel, which is extremely rare for Patek Philippe watches, and it is adorned with intricate decorations and engravings. The watch is powered by two independent movements, each with its own barrel, and it has a power reserve of 72 hours. It is also water-resistant to 30 meters and comes with a brown leather strap and a stainless-steel bracelet. The Patek Philippe Grandmaster Chime Ref. 6300A-010 is considered a masterpiece of watchmaking, and its sale broke the record for the most expensive watch ever sold at auction. It was purchased by an anonymous bidder, who undoubtedly appreciated its unique design and exceptional craftsmanship. And who said time is money? Well, apparently, for the lucky anonymous bidder, it's $31 million!

78. The idea of wearing a wedding veil comes from ancient Greece and Rome, where it was believed to protect the bride from evil spirits.

The tradition of wearing a wedding veil has a long and rich history. One of the earliest records of wearing a wedding veil comes from ancient Greece and Rome, where brides wore a veil made of flame-colored, bright yellow or deep red fabric, known as a flammeum. The flammeum was meant to ward off evil spirits, and to symbolize the bride's willingness to enter into the marriage contract. In medieval times, the wedding veil was a symbol of modesty and chastity. It was believed that the veil helped to conceal the bride's face from the groom until after the ceremony was completed, thus helping to ensure that the couple was not entering into the marriage for superficial reasons. As time went on, the wedding veil became a symbol of purity, innocence, and virginity. The white wedding veil that we know today became popular in the 19th century, after Queen Victoria of England wore a white veil at her wedding to Prince Albert in 1840. This sparked a trend among upper-class brides in Europe and North America, and the white wedding veil became a symbol of purity and innocence. In some cultures, the wedding veil has additional symbolism. In Jewish tradition, the bride wears a veil during the ceremony to show that her beauty is reserved for her husband alone. In Islamic tradition, the bride may wear a hijab or a full-face veil as a sign of respect and modesty. Despite its long history and various meanings, one thing is for sure: a wedding veil is a bride's best accessory for hiding happy tears during the ceremony!

79.   The first fashion magazine is said to be "Cabinet des Modes", a French fashion magazine that was published from 1785 to 1793.

"Cabinet des Modes" was considered to be the first women's fashion magazine ever published, and it featured illustrations of the latest fashion trends from the top designers of the time. The magazine was aimed at the upper classes of French society, and it quickly became a must-read publication for those who wanted to stay up-to-date with the latest styles and trends. One of the unique aspects of "Cabinet des Modes" was the fact that it was published in small, pocket-sized volumes that were easy to carry around. This made it convenient for women to take the magazine with them to dressmakers and designers, allowing them to easily show them the latest trends they wanted to incorporate into their own wardrobes. The magazine was published by a group of women who called themselves the "Société des Amateurs de Modes." They were passionate about fashion and wanted to create a publication that would showcase the latest trends and designs. The magazine was published in both French and English, which helped to expand its readership beyond France to other countries in Europe and even America. The success of "Cabinet des Modes" paved the way for many other fashion magazines that followed, and it remains an important milestone in the history of fashion journalism. And for those who can't keep up with the latest fashion trends, there's always the "just wear whatever is clean" magazine - it's a bestseller among busy parents and procrastinators everywhere!

80. The buttons on men's and women's shirts are placed on opposite sides. This originates from the fact that wealthy women were often dressed by their maids, who would face them while buttoning up their clothing.

The tradition of placing buttons on opposite sides of men's and women's clothing dates back to the 16th century. At that time, clothing was expensive and difficult to produce, so it was common for both men and women to wear garments that were essentially unisex in design. However, as fashion began to evolve and clothing became more tailored to the individual wearer, subtle differences emerged between men's and women's garments. One of these differences was the placement of buttons. For men, buttons were typically placed on the right side of the garment, while women's buttons were placed on the left. One of the most widely accepted theories is that it was related to the practice of dressing. In the past, it was common for wealthy women to have a maid or servant who would assist them with dressing. Since most people are right-handed, it was easier for a maid to button up a woman's clothing if the buttons were placed on the left side. This would allow the maid to stand in front of the woman and use her right hand to button up the garment. For men, on the other hand, buttoning up clothing was typically done without assistance, so it made sense to place the buttons on the right side, where they could be easily reached by the wearer's right hand. Over time, this tradition became so ingrained that it is now a standard feature of men's and women's clothing. And for those who still can't figure out which side the buttons should be on, there's always the "just wear a zipper" option - it's foolproof!

17. POLITICS

81. The United States is one of the few countries in the world where its citizens pledge allegiance to the national flag.

In the United States, the Pledge of Allegiance is a well-known symbol of patriotism and loyalty to the country. The pledge is recited daily in many schools and public institutions and is often associated with national events such as Independence Day or Veterans Day. The current version of the pledge was adopted in 1954 and reads: "I pledge allegiance to the Flag of the United States of America, and to the Republic for which it stands, one Nation under God, indivisible, with liberty and justice for all." While the pledge is optional and not legally required, it has been a contentious issue throughout American history. Some have argued that it is a violation of individual liberties to require citizens to pledge allegiance to the flag, while others see it as a way to instill a sense of national pride and unity. In contrast, many other countries have different approaches to the concept of allegiance. In the United Kingdom and Canada, for example, there is an oath of allegiance — a promise or declaration of fealty to the monarch (as personification of the state and its authority, rather than as an individual person). Overall, the concept of pledging allegiance reflects a country's values and identity, and it can be an important symbol of national unity and pride. But let's be honest, most people just try to mumble through the "indivisible" part without tripping over their tongues!

82. The country of Bhutan measures its success in terms of "Gross National Happiness" instead of the more common "Gross Domestic Product" (GDP).

Bhutan is a small landlocked country in South Asia that is known for measuring its success through a unique concept known as Gross National Happiness (GNH). The concept was developed in the 1970s by the Fourth King of Bhutan, Jigme Singye Wangchuck, who believed that the country's development should not be based solely on economic growth, but should also take into account the well-being and happiness of its citizens. The GNH index measures the country's progress using four pillars: sustainable and equitable economic growth, preservation and promotion of cultural values, conservation of the environment, and good governance. These pillars are further divided into nine domains, which include factors such as education, health, living standards, community vitality, and psychological well-being. In 2011, the United Nations adopted a resolution that recognized happiness as a fundamental human goal and called for the promotion of policies that increase the well-being of people around the world. Although Bhutan is a small country with a relatively low GDP, its focus on GNH has resulted in a strong sense of community, a healthy environment, and a high level of citizen satisfaction. Bhutan's success in promoting happiness and well-being has made it a model for other countries to follow, and has highlighted the importance of considering factors beyond economic growth in measuring progress. With such a focus on happiness and well-being, it's no wonder that Bhutan is known as the Land of Smiles!

83. The Vatican City, the smallest country in the world, has no prison. Criminals are instead transferred to Italian prisons for their sentences.

The Vatican City is a sovereign city-state located in the heart of Rome, Italy, and is the smallest country in the world, both by size and population. It has a unique status as an independent city-state and is home to the Pope, who serves as the head of the Roman Catholic Church. Despite being an independent country, the Vatican City has no prison of its own. Instead, it relies on Italy to provide prison facilities for those who commit crimes within its borders. This arrangement is due to the small size of the Vatican City, as it does not have the resources or the space to operate its own prison system. The Vatican City does, however, have its own police force, known as the Vatican Gendarmerie, which is responsible for maintaining law and order within the city-state. In cases where a crime is committed, the Vatican Gendarmerie will investigate and apprehend the suspect, who will then be transferred to an Italian prison to serve their sentence. It is worth noting that the Vatican City has a low crime rate, due in part to its small population and the high level of security within its borders. The Vatican Gendarmerie is responsible for protecting the Pope, as well as the many priceless treasures and artworks housed within the city-state. So, if you're planning on committing a crime, maybe avoid doing it in the Vatican City. Not only because it's morally wrong, but because you'll end up spending your jail time in an Italian prison with no access to holy water or rosaries!

84. The title "czar" or "tsar" used by the rulers of Russia until 1917 actually comes from the Latin word "Caesar," as they saw themselves as the heirs to the Roman Empire.

The title "czar" or "tsar" is derived from the word "Caesar," which was the title given to the rulers of ancient Rome. The rulers of Russia adopted the title in the late 15th century and used it until the Russian Revolution in 1917. The czars saw themselves as the successors of the Roman emperors and therefore adopted the title of Caesar to emphasize their connection to the ancient Roman Empire. The first Russian ruler to use the title was Ivan IV, also known as Ivan the Terrible, who was crowned czar in 1547. Over time, the title became synonymous with absolute power and authority. The czars were considered to be divinely appointed and were believed to have complete control over their subjects. The last czar of Russia was Nicholas II, who was overthrown in the Russian Revolution of 1917. After his abdication, he and his family were imprisoned by the Bolsheviks and eventually executed in 1918. With the end of the Russian monarchy, the title of czar was abolished and replaced by a Soviet government. Perhaps Nicholas II should have taken a cue from Julius Caesar and beware the Ides of March!

85.   The tiny island nation of Nauru has the world's highest level of obesity, with over 60% of its population considered to be obese. This is partly due to the country's reliance on imported processed foods, as well as a lack of exercise options on the small island.

Nauru is a small island nation located in the Pacific Ocean, northeast of Australia. It has a population of around 10,000 people and covers an area of just 21 square kilometers. Despite its small size, Nauru has the dubious distinction of having the world's highest level of obesity, with over 60% of its population considered to be obese. The high rate of obesity in Nauru is due to a number of factors, including a lack of exercise options, limited access to fresh fruits and vegetables, and a reliance on imported processed foods. The country has a very limited agricultural sector and most of its food is imported, leading to a diet that is high in sugar, fat, and processed foods. Nauru has also faced a number of health challenges in recent years, including a rise in cases of diabetes, heart disease, and other obesity-related conditions. The country has limited healthcare resources, which makes it difficult to address these health issues effectively. Efforts are being made to combat the high rates of obesity in Nauru, including initiatives to promote healthy eating and exercise, and to reduce the consumption of processed foods. However, these efforts face significant challenges due to the limited resources available in the country. But on the plus side, Nauruans are experts in creating deliciously unhealthy snacks, so if you're ever in the mood for a deep-fried, sugar-coated treat, you know where to go!

18. ASTRONOMY & SPACE

86. Astronauts in space grow up to 2 inches (5 cm) taller because the lack of gravity allows the spine to elongate.

Astronauts experience a number of physiological changes due to the effects of microgravity on the human body, and one of the most notable is a temporary increase in height. In a weightless environment, the spine no longer has to support the weight of the body, which can cause the discs between the vertebrae to expand. This expansion can result in an increase in height of up to 2 inches (5 cm) for some astronauts. However, this increase in height is only temporary, as the spine will return to its original length once the astronaut returns to Earth and experiences the effects of gravity once again. The process of returning to normal height can be somewhat uncomfortable, as the spine compresses again and the astronaut may experience a sensation similar to the feeling of having their back pressed together. The increase in height is just one of the many changes that astronauts experience while in space. Other physiological changes include muscle atrophy, bone loss, changes in the cardiovascular system, and changes in the immune system. But on the bright side, for those who have always dreamed of being taller, space travel might be the perfect solution. Just don't get too attached to those extra 2 inches!

87. The planet Venus spins in the opposite direction to all the other planets in our solar system.

Out of the eight planets in our solar system, Venus is the only planet that rotates in a clockwise or retrograde direction, while all other planets, including Earth, rotate counterclockwise. This means that if you were standing on the surface of Venus, the sun would rise in the west and set in the east, opposite to what we observe on Earth. The reason for this strange behavior is still not completely understood, but scientists believe it could be due to a large collision or gravitational interactions with other objects in the early solar system. Another theory is that the thick atmosphere of Venus may have caused the planet to slow down and eventually reverse its rotation over time. Venus is also unique in other ways, such as having the hottest surface temperature of any planet in the solar system, with temperatures reaching up to 864 degrees Fahrenheit (462 degrees Celsius) due to its dense atmosphere and greenhouse effect. The planet is often referred to as Earth's "sister planet" due to its similar size and composition, but its extreme conditions make it a challenging place for exploration and study. But hey, at least on Venus you'll never be late for a sunrise!

88. The temperature in space varies widely depending on location.

Space is an incredibly vast and varied environment, with temperatures that can vary widely depending on the location and conditions. In the shadow of a celestial body, temperatures can drop to incredibly low levels. For example, in the shadow of the Moon, temperatures can drop to as low as -173°C (-280°F). Similarly, temperatures in the shadow of a planet or moon can reach as low as -270°C (-454°F), making it one of the coldest places in the universe. On the other hand, temperatures in direct sunlight can soar to incredibly high levels. In fact, the temperature on the surface of the Sun itself is around 5,500°C (9,932°F). However, even in space, temperatures can reach extremely high levels due to the presence of highly energetic particles and radiation. For example, the temperature of the solar wind, which is the stream of particles flowing from the Sun, can reach over 1,000,000°C (1,800,032°F) in some areas. The temperature in space can also vary depending on the time of day or the season. For example, the temperature on the Moon can vary by as much as 300°C (540°F) between its day and night sides. This is because the Moon has no atmosphere to regulate its temperature and thus its surface temperature can vary widely depending on its exposure to sunlight. Another interesting fact is that it can vary depending on the location in the universe. For example, the temperature of the cosmic microwave background radiation is only around -270°C (-454°F) today, a result of the expansion of the universe which has caused the radiation to cool over time. So, if you're planning a space vacation, make sure to pack both your sunscreen and your parka!

89. Gaia BH1 is the nearest known system that astronomers are reasonably confident contains a black hole.

Gaia BH1 is a system in the Milky Way galaxy that is believed to contain a black hole. It was discovered by the European Space Agency's Gaia satellite, which is used to measure the positions, distances, and motions of stars in the Milky Way. The system is located 1,560 light-years (478 pc) away from the Solar System in the constellation of Ophiuchus, making it one of the closest known black hole systems to our planet. However, the presence of the black hole has not been directly confirmed, as astronomers have not been able to observe the black hole itself. Instead, they have inferred its existence based on the motion of the stars in the system. Gaia BH1 is thought to contain a black hole with a mass of around 9.62 times that of the sun. Studying black hole systems like Gaia BH1 is important for astronomers to understand the behavior and properties of these enigmatic objects, which are known for their extreme gravitational pull and ability to warp spacetime. But don't worry, the chances of us getting sucked into a black hole anytime soon are about as likely as winning the lottery while being struck by lightning and attacked by a shark all at the same time!

90. There is a planet called HD 189733b that rains glass sideways in its atmosphere, with winds of up to 8,700 kilometers per hour (5,400 mph).

HD 189733b is an exoplanet located approximately 63 light-years away from Earth in the constellation of Vulpecula. It was discovered in 2005 and is about the same size as Jupiter, but orbits much closer to its parent star, HD 189733. As a result, the planet is extremely hot, with surface temperatures reaching up to 2,000 degrees Celsius (3,632 degrees Fahrenheit). The high temperatures and strong winds on HD 189733b create a unique phenomenon where it "rains" glass sideways in its atmosphere. The winds on the planet can reach up to 8,700 kilometers per hour (5,400 mph), which is about seven times the speed of sound on Earth. These winds are generated by the extreme heating and cooling of the planet's atmosphere, which causes strong, hurricane-like storms that whip across the surface. The glass that rains down on HD 189733b is formed from silicates in the planet's atmosphere that are heated to extreme temperatures and then condense into small, molten droplets. As these droplets are carried by the strong winds, they cool and solidify into tiny, glassy particles that rain down sideways onto the planet's surface. This phenomenon was first detected in 2013 using NASA's Hubble Space Telescope. Overall, HD 189733b is an intriguing and extreme world that provides valuable insights into the complex and diverse nature of planets beyond our solar system. And if you thought your daily commute was bad, imagine having to dodge raining glass at 8,700 kph (5,400 mph)!

19. MISCELLANEOUS

91. The longest interval between the birth of twins is 97 days.

In November 2018, a set of twins were born 97 days apart in Cologne, Germany. The first twin, named Liana, was born prematurely at 26 weeks and weighed just 790 grams. Doctors placed her in intensive care and worked hard to keep her alive. Meanwhile, Liana's mother, Oxana, continued to carry her sister, Leonie, in the womb. During the following weeks, Leonie continued to grow and develop normally. However, Liana faced numerous health complications, including sepsis and a serious lung infection. Despite these challenges, Liana slowly began to improve and was eventually released from the hospital after three months. Surprisingly, after Liana was discharged from the hospital, her mother did not go into labor for another 12 weeks. On February 23, 2019, 97 days after Liana's birth, her sister Leonie was born. Leonie was born at full term and weighed a healthy 3.9 kilograms (8.6 pounds). The birth of the twins 97 days apart is an incredibly rare occurrence and is believed to be one of the longest intervals between the birth of twins. The twins' parents were overjoyed to have both of their daughters home and healthy after such a difficult journey. Who knew that being fashionably late started in the womb?

92. The shortest commercial flight in the world is between two Scottish islands, Westray and Papa Westray. The flight takes only 53 seconds and covers a distance of just 2.7 kilometers (1.7 miles).

The Westray to Papa Westray flight, operated by Loganair, is the shortest scheduled passenger flight in the world. It takes only 53 seconds to cover the distance between the two Scottish islands, which are located in the Orkney Islands archipelago, north of mainland Scotland. The flight was first launched in 1967 and has been in operation ever since, serving as a vital link between the two islands. The flight is typically operated using a Britten-Norman Islander aircraft, which can carry up to eight passengers at a time. The flight is so short that passengers barely have time to buckle their seatbelts before the plane lands. Despite its short duration, the flight is considered to be a unique and memorable experience by those who have taken it. It offers stunning views of the Scottish coastline and is a popular attraction for aviation enthusiasts from around the world. The cost of the flight is relatively inexpensive, making it accessible to anyone who wants to experience this one-of-a-kind travel experience. Overall, the Westray to Papa Westray flight is a testament to the ingenuity and resourcefulness of those who live in remote areas of the world, who have found innovative ways to connect with each other and the rest of the world. And if you're not careful, you might miss the flight altogether - just make sure you don't blink during takeoff!

93. The longest continuous sidewalk in the world is located in Rio de Janeiro, Brazil. The Copacabana Beach sidewalk stretches for 4.15 kilometers (2.58 miles) and is a popular destination for tourists and locals alike.

The Copacabana Beach sidewalk, also known as Avenida Atlântica, is an iconic landmark of Rio de Janeiro and a popular tourist attraction. The sidewalk runs parallel to the sandy beach, and offers stunning views of the Atlantic Ocean and the surrounding mountains. It was constructed in the 1930s and has undergone several renovations since then to improve its quality and accessibility. The sidewalk is divided into two lanes, one for pedestrians and the other for cyclists. Along the sidewalk, visitors can find a variety of amenities such as kiosks selling food and drinks, souvenir shops, and street performers. The area is particularly lively during the annual Rio Carnival, when it serves as a parade route for samba schools. Despite its popularity, the Copacabana Beach sidewalk has faced challenges over the years. The area is prone to flooding during heavy rains, and there have been efforts to improve the drainage system to mitigate this issue. In addition, the beach and sidewalk have been impacted by erosion, leading to beach replenishment projects to restore the shoreline. Overall, the Copacabana Beach sidewalk is a beloved part of Rio de Janeiro and serves as a gathering place for people from all walks of life. If you're feeling adventurous, you can try to walk the entire length of the Copacabana Beach sidewalk. But be warned, it might take you longer than you think - with all the distractions along the way, you might end up spending more time snacking and people-watching than actually moving forward!

94. The jigsaw with the greatest number of pieces had 551,232 pieces and measured 14.85 × 23.20 m (48 ft 8.64 in × 76 ft 1.38 in). It was assembled on 25 September 2011 at Phú Thọ Indoor Stadium in Ho Chi Minh City, Vietnam.

The jigsaw puzzle, also known as "Memorable Disney Moments," was created by the Vietnamese company, V&A Group, and features 10 different classic Disney scenes. The completed puzzle weighs over 1,600 pounds and took over 17 days to assemble by a team of 20 people. The puzzle was certified by Guinness World Records as the largest jigsaw puzzle ever made, breaking the previous record of 551,232 pieces held by a puzzle named "Keith Haring: Double Retrospect," which had 32,256 pieces less. The completed puzzle was put on display at the exhibition hall of the Tan Binh Exhibition & Convention Center in Ho Chi Minh City, where it drew large crowds of curious visitors from all over the world. The puzzle's enormous size and intricate design make it not only a remarkable feat of engineering but also a unique work of art that celebrates the enduring appeal of Disney's beloved characters and stories. But don't be fooled, the real challenge isn't assembling the puzzle, it's finding a table large enough to fit it!

95. The national flag of Nepal is the only flag in the world that is not rectangular or square in shape.

The Nepalese flag is a symbol of the country's history and cultural identity. It was first adopted on December 16, 1962, although it had been used by the Nepalese Army since the 19th century. The flag's unique shape is also significant, as two overlapping triangles represent the nation's commitment to unity and harmony between different cultures and religions. The blue border around the flag symbolizes peace and stability, while the crimson red color represents the courage of the Nepalese people. The flag's design has undergone several modifications over the years, but the basic elements of the two triangles and the border have remained unchanged. The Nepalese flag is also steeped in symbolism, with each color and shape having a specific meaning. The white moon on the upper triangle represents the royal family, while the white sun on the lower triangle represents the Rana family, who held power in Nepal from the mid-19th century until the early 20th century. The two triangles also represent the country's two major religions, with the lower triangle representing the more numerous Hindu population, and the upper triangle representing the Buddhist minority. The flag is a source of great pride for the Nepalese people and is displayed prominently on all official buildings and at national events. Interestingly, due to the flag's shape, it cannot be easily produced by conventional flag makers, and therefore, many of the Nepalese flags sold around the world are actually rectangular imitations. So, if you want to get a real Nepalese flag, make sure to look for the one with the pointy ends!

AND...

20. TOILETS

**96.   a. The city of Uruk in Iraq exhibits the earliest known internal pit toilet from c. 3200 BC.
b. The modern flush toilet was invented in 1596 by Sir John Harrington.
c. The development of high-tech toilets can be traced back to the early 1980s in Japan.**

a. The city of Uruk, located in modern-day Warka in southern Iraq, is considered to have had one of the earliest urban civilizations in the world, dating back to around 4000 BC. As part of this urbanization, the city had a sophisticated sewage system that included the earliest known internal pit toilet dating back to around 3200 BC. The toilet was constructed of brick and consisted of a seat with a hole, which led to a pit below. Waste was collected in the pit, which was then periodically emptied by workers who carried the waste out of the city. This early development of toilets and sewage systems played a crucial role in promoting hygiene and public health in ancient cities. And to think, all of this time we thought indoor plumbing was a modern invention!

b. Sir John Harrington's invention of the modern flush toilet in 1596 was initially intended for Queen Elizabeth I's private use at her palace in Richmond, England. The device was nicknamed the "Ajax" after the hero in Greek mythology who was known for his strength and agility. Despite Harrington's innovation, it took several centuries for flush toilets to become widely adopted. The first water closet was introduced in 1738, and it wasn't until the mid-19th century that indoor plumbing and modern toilets became more common in households. Thomas Crapper, a British plumber and inventor, is often credited with popularizing the modern toilet in the late 1800s, but this is actually a myth. While Crapper did make some important contributions to the development of the modern toilet, including the ballcock mechanism that controls the flow of water into the tank, he did not invent the toilet itself. It seems that Sir John Harrington's "Ajax" invention was truly ahead of its time, taking centuries for the rest of society to catch up and embrace this essential piece of modern plumbing. As for Thomas Crapper, it turns out he wasn't the "Number 1" inventor of the toilet after all!

c. Since the 1980s, high-tech toilets have become increasingly popular in many countries, particularly Japan. These toilets offer a range of features beyond traditional toilets, given that some models can even analyze urine and stool samples for signs of disease or infection, while others measure blood pressure, temperature, and blood sugar levels. These features make high-tech toilets a symbol of technological advancement and a way to enhance personal hygiene. The toilets are designed to provide maximum convenience and hygiene for users, with a variety of automated features, including self-cleaning mechanisms, rotating toilet seats, water jets or "bottom washers" for cleaning, blow dryers and even music to help mask any sounds. Who knew that using the bathroom could be such a musical experience? Just make sure you're hitting all the right notes!

97. A 2009 study conducted in Israel found that a majority of adults read from their cell phones on the toilet.

The study, which was conducted by a team of researchers from the University of Haifa, surveyed 1,000 Israelis about their toilet habits. The researchers found that 90% of respondents reported using their cell phones while on the toilet, with nearly three-quarters saying they sent text messages and emails. The study also found that women were more likely than men to use their phones while on the toilet, and that people under 30 were the most frequent users. While the study was limited to Israel, it's likely that similar trends can be found in other countries. With the widespread use of smartphones and other mobile devices, it has become increasingly common for people to bring their devices with them to the bathroom, including the toilet. However, as previously mentioned, spending too long seated on the toilet may contribute to issues like hemorrhoids, since the position increases strain on the rectal veins. Overall, while reading or using a cell phone on the toilet may seem like a harmless habit, it's important to be aware of the potential health risks and to limit time spent on the toilet. While the study found that using a cell phone on the toilet is a popular habit, it's worth noting that it can also lead to "crappy" phone hygiene if not properly disinfected!

98. The psychoanalyst Otto Fenichel believed bathroom reading was an indication of early childhood trauma.

Otto Fenichel was an Austrian psychoanalyst who was particularly interested in the developmental psychology of children. Fenichel believed that the origins of adult behavior and neuroses could be traced back to early childhood experiences. According to him, bathroom reading was a sign of an individual's unresolved feelings of loss related to toilet training. He suggested that children who had a difficult time during toilet training might find solace in reading while on the toilet, as it provides a sense of control and a way to cope with the stress of the experience. While there is no scientific evidence to support Fenichel's theory, it is still an interesting idea to consider. Many people find that reading in the bathroom is a way to escape from the stresses of everyday life and can be a form of self-care. However, it is important to note that excessive bathroom reading could potentially be a sign of avoidance behavior and may be indicative of an underlying issue that should be addressed. Overall, while Fenichel's theory on bathroom reading and early childhood trauma may not be widely accepted by the scientific community, it is an interesting perspective to consider when examining the reasons behind this common practice. And for those of us who enjoy reading on the toilet, perhaps we should just blame our parents for any unresolved feelings of loss related to potty training!

99. The term "bathroom reading" refers to any literary material deemed suitable for casual or light reading.

The term "bathroom reading" is commonly used to refer to reading material that is entertaining or informative but not necessarily intellectually challenging. Such material is often found in books, magazines, and newspapers that are placed in bathrooms for guests to peruse while using the facilities. The content of bathroom reading material can range from humorous anecdotes to trivia and puzzles, and it can be tailored to different audiences based on their interests. The origins of bathroom reading are unclear, but it is believed to have become popular in the United States during the 20th century. One theory is that it originated in public restrooms, where newspapers were placed for patrons to read while using the facilities. Over time, the practice spread to private homes, where books and magazines were placed in bathrooms as a form of light entertainment. While some may view bathroom reading as a trivial activity, others argue that it serves a valuable purpose in promoting reading and literacy. Reading while on the toilet can provide a brief escape from the stresses of daily life and offer a moment of relaxation. It can also provide a source of intellectual stimulation and help individuals stay informed about current events and popular culture. So next time you're feeling bored on the throne, remember that you're not alone in your love for bathroom reading – it's a time-honored tradition that's here to stay!

100. Reading on the toilet can actually lead to hemorrhoids. Sitting on the toilet for long periods of time puts pressure on the veins in the rectum, which can cause hemorrhoids to form. To avoid this, it's best to limit time spent on the toilet and avoid reading while sitting.

Hemorrhoids are swollen veins in the lower rectum and anus, and they can be painful and uncomfortable. Prolonged sitting on the toilet, especially if you strain while trying to have a bowel movement, can increase the risk of developing hemorrhoids. While reading on the toilet is a common habit, it can actually worsen the condition by causing you to sit for longer periods of time. To reduce the risk of developing hemorrhoids, it is recommended to use a footstool to raise your feet, avoid straining during bowel movements, increase fiber intake, stay hydrated, and, of course, limit time spent reading on the toilet. Our advice? One page, one wipe!

978-618-86745-0-9

More from the author:

Legal deposit: July 2023
ISBN: 978-618-86745-0-9